TEA WITHOUT SUGAR

CHASTENED FOR A DESTINY

Powerful Testimonies by
Discipleship College Graduates
as told to Dr Marcia Anderso

TEA WITHOUT SUGAR:

CHASTENED FOR A DESTINY

By Graduates of Discipleship College
As Told To
Dr. Marcia R. Anderson

Discipleship College
Eldoret, Kenya
2012, 2016

Printed by:
Utafiti Foundation
Pioneer Estate, Off Kapsabet Road,
P. O. Box 884 – 30100, Eldoret, Kenya.
Tel: +254-053-206-302-4
Website: www.utafitifoundation.com
Copy-righted 2012 by Marcia R. Anderson. Revised and enlarged, 2016.
ISBN: 978-1-59684-724-

FOREWORD

Have you ever read true stories told by real people that caused you to marvel how God works phenomenally to bring to fruition his purpose? Tea Without Sugar is a collection of true stories of former Discipleship College students as told to Dr. Marcia, a lecturer at Discipleship College in Eldoret, Kenya. Reading these stories one gets to see how God is actively involved and in charge of our lives. The stories provoke one's mind to do an inventory of his or her personal journey and see that God has indeed led them to their current destination. This is one of the books you will read and appreciate how God is at work even when we are oblivious of His work and presence.

Many people have referred to Africa as a dark continent, a continent from which God has probably turned his face. However, the stories in this book testify to the contrary. Indeed reading these stories one gets to see the God who is at work in Africa, recruiting an army for Himself, albeit in very diverse and unique ways and in different circumstances.

The story tellers come from different countries of East Africa; namely, Sudan, Kenya, and Uganda. Dr. Marcia hopes that through these stories that many Christians outside of Africa will get a glimpse of what God is doing and be challenged to participate in the development of leaders that God is calling to serve their own nations in Africa.

Dr. Marcia is a passionate missionary teacher who has sold herself totally to the work of God. One of the challenges she has often encountered is seeing men and women who are EVIDENTLY called by God miss out on the opportunity to be trained simply for lack of financial resources. Dr. Marcia put together these stories at the urging of the Holy Spirit as a call to all to partner with her in developing workers for Christ in Africa here at Discipleship College.

May you have a wonderful time reading, reflecting and praying for Africa!

James Kagari
Academic Dean,
Discipleship College, Eldoret, Kenya.
January, 2012

Discipleship College was started to train church leaders for East Africa. It is owned and operated by Church of God World Missions but is open to any believer who has no hesitation about studying in a Pentecostal setting. The stories you are about to read reflect the openness of the student body. These stories will leave you laughing, crying and wondering at God's Grace and man's determination to follow God at any cost. May these stories inspire you and give you courage to be all God wants you to be in His Kingdom. He has all the circumstances of your life in His Hands.

Gordon Bloodworth
Founder and Associate Professor Emeritus,
Discipleship College, Eldoret, Kenya.
January, 2012

With this book Dr. Marcia has given a priceless gift to the literary world; the deeply personal stories of lives of Christians in an impoverished arena. They are true stories that unveil a world unknown to a foreigner. True accounts of fear, lack, distress, and endurance captivate the attention of the reader.

The connecting thread in these remarkable stories is God's miraculous ways of protection, deliverance, guidance and faithfulness to open doors for His children. Starkly shocking facts will inspire and challenge Christians everywhere to look deep within, questioning their own spiritual commitment if faced with the same obstacles.

Jeanette Chesser
Guest Lecturer and Short Term Missionary,
Discipleship College, Eldoret, Kenya.
Ocala, Florida, January, 2012

DEDICATION

This revised edition of *Tea Without Sugar* is dedicated to Waneda Brownlow, long-time missionary and dear friend of the "listener" to these stories. She loved the college and was a great encouragement to me in the compiling of these stories. I believe she would rejoice to see two more countries: Ethiopia and Rwanda, represented among the stories of *Tea Without Sugar*. Waneda served for six years as Coordinator of Children's Ministries in all of Africa for Church of God World Missions, Cleveland, Tennessee. After a serious bout with cancer eight years before, she had asked her Lord Jesus for six more years on the mission field. He gave them to her. She went to be with the Lord on August 24, 2014.

The first edition was edited by Waneda as a member of the Ministerial Development Fund which provided scholarships at Discipleship College. All of the proceeds of this fund went to help deserving students at the college. The life stories of two of those recipients are included in this extended edition. They are Gezahegn Amare and Janvier Nsanzumuhire. I know she would want you to enjoy these stories and would rejoice that more students like Gezahegn and Janvier will benefit from the proceeds of this latest edition as this volume's proceeds go to Discipleship College's scholarship fund.

Marcia Anderson,
Eldoret, Kenya, 2016

PREFACE

The title of this book was birthed in a conversation with one of the contributors to this book. As he was walking to my house (Marcia) to talk to me about this book he was thinking about people who were feeling very discouraged because of the rising cost of sugar. To have "chai" – Kenyan tea – without sugar is to these people an unthinkable hardship. My friend immediately began to think of the times when he had no tea at all, when to have even "black" tea (without milk and sugar) would have been a great gift. Then he began to reflect on how God had used hard, painful times in his life to prepare him for his destiny.

We realized together that there is a common thread in these stories. Great obstacles have had to be overcome by each one of these who have shared their stories. Each of them has sensed a divine purpose in their lives and without exception, they have seen that God has used each trial, each difficulty, to fit them for His higher purposes – that they might fulfill the destiny He has prepared for them. And so the title of this book is

TEA WITHOUT SUGAR: CHASTENED FOR A DESTINY.

Students come and go, but those who remain, who persevere to the end, are a special precious group, who have learned that suffering and affliction - the chastening of the Lord - come to all who are called to follow Him. This chastening is not without purpose. Indeed, people throughout the world suffer incredible hardships and often do not understand any purpose beyond that suffering. But these choice instruments of God's purpose understand that suffering is not the end. They have learned the amazing presence of the Lord in the midst of affliction and have already glimpsed the glory of the Destiny to which they are called.

There are many others who could have been included in this collection, but these stories are representative of the students I have met in Kenya. If we missed your story this time, there may be another book!

It is our prayer, that as you read these powerful testimonies your heart will be filled with gratitude for the hard things in your life as well as the "sugar" and that you will have renewed courage to walk forward into your own destiny.

CONTENTS

Foreword i

Dedication... iii

Preface iv

Contents v

Chapter 1: *Tears that Heal* - Abraham Lual Panchol 1

Chapter 2: *Care for the Fish!* - Christopher Mujesia Chiveyia 9

Chapter 3: *Pregnant for 18 Months!* - Mary Nakalembe Kyalagamba
.... 22

Chapter 4: *Life after Genocide* - Janvier Nsanzumuhire 26

Chapter 5: *Listen to the Small Boy* - Davis M. Gatua 35

Chapter 6: *Soap is Enough!* - Jairus Mosoti 40

Chapter 7: *Lost Boy* - Gabriel Chol Pareng 60

Chapter 8: *Snatched from a Cult* - Nicas Wasike Nyakuri 68

Chapter 9: *A Bit of a Fool* - Gezahegn Amare 79

Chapter 10: *Deadly Diagnosis* - Petronilla Mbakaya 93

Chapter 11: *Head to Toe* - Peter Mwaura Ndungu 102

Chapter 12: *Free Behind Bars* - Titus Etiang 113

Chapter 13: *A Piece of Charcoal* - John Kagwe 136

Chapter 14: *His Grace is Sufficient* - Paul Kipng'etich Cheboswony 151

Chapter 15: *Expelled to Excel* - Lawrence Ouma Osewe 161

Chapter 16: *Til Death Do Us Part: Our Story* - Flojo Sikobe 169

Epilogue: *A Last Sip of Tea* - D. E. "Gene" Mills, Jr. 187

Glossary of Terms 189

Tea Without Sugar: Chastened for a Destiny

TEARS THAT HEAL
Abraham Lual Panchol

I remember when the visions began. I was only 6 years old. The year was 1982. I felt the devil – he was very dark with long horns. He came to spear me. I cried out for help and I told the people around me – my dad and my mom – "I saw a witch!" My father and mom asked me, "Where is the witch?" I said, "It was right here." But I was the only one who saw him; the rest of the people didn't see anything, so they thought maybe I had malaria and was hallucinating. The next morning my younger sister fell sick and by 5 pm in the evening she was dead. People were thinking to take her to the mortuary in Bor town, but my grandmom refused, saying, "No, we will take her tomorrow." That evening, I refused to eat; instead, I cried. I cried until morning, and do you know what happened? My sister was raised from the dead. People were not praying or doing anything concerning her with their idols. Only I cried and sang a song I heard in the church which said, "Jesus is my future, He died for me!"

You see, my mom and dad were nominal Christians, and so, no one believed that Jesus had raised her from the dead except me. My father was a Christian in name only; he smoked and drank and lived like the world. I think you would call him a carnal Christian. Mother also was not "born again" and didn't expect something like this to happen. Somehow, they thought my crying was heard by God, but they did not acknowledge that Jesus was the healer. My grandmother, in particular, didn't know Christ. For me, this was the first sign which I had seen in my life that Jesus performed. Twenty years later people acknowledged that it was Jesus who raised her up. At that time my father was very sick, at the point of death, and Jesus confronted him in his comatose state and said, "You did not thank me for raising your daughter." Jesus told me to call all my father's sons to pray for him. After our father saw that vision and we prayed for him, he came back

Tea Without Sugar: Chastened for a Destiny

to life. Then he acknowledged that Jesus had healed my little sister, too.

When I was born my father gave me the name of Abraham because there was a man named Abraham who was a priest in our area; in fact, he was the first man in our area who believed in Jesus. He prophesied that my father would have a son named Abraham and that I would be a priest.

Soon after my father named me, I was dedicated to the Lord in the Anglican church. But I was not baptized until 1987, when I was 8 years old. I was baptized by Pastor Jacob Mayom Abui, a Pentecostal pastor. A year after my baptism, I had a dream. Somebody came to me with water and gave me a drink. The one who gave me the water was a white man and he called himself, "Bob." He told me that this water would rise in my heart as eternal life. When I saw that vision, I started eagerly to read the Bible in the Dinka Bor language. No one taught me. We were still learning the ABC's in English in school. At that time I began to preach the gospel. By the time I was 12 years old (1990), I had planted two churches in my village, which are still existing. One church has a high deacon and the other church has a priest. I guess you would say that in that process, I became an evangelist.

The life of an evangelist is not easy. Sometimes people misunderstand what you are doing. For example, in my appointment as an evangelist, I traveled from place to place in Southern Sudan. During the war this was very risky. Once, at the time for Christmas celebrations in the church, I had a problem—my cow was stolen. There was nobody willing to look for it because there were many people stealing cattle at that time. I knew the man who took my cow. Instead of beginning to look for the cow, I began to pray because I didn't know where to search. I fasted for one 24-hour day, from one morning until the next morning. As I prayed, I was lifted up by the Holy Spirit and I heard the words, "Just go to Juba Abui; that's where your cow is." It was a cattle camp. I went out looking for that camp. When I reached the place, I saw my cow, who now had a calf. Those men who were in that cattle camp were against the government of the SPLA (Sudan People's Liberation Army). Because the SPLA was dominated by Dinkas and I am Dinka, when I reached the cattle camp and claimed my cow, they refused to return it to me. These men were from the Mundare and I did not know how to speak their language of Bhari, so I spoke to them in Arabic. Instead of giving me my cow, they started to beat me. They wanted to kill me. They had been told (because I was well-dressed), "Just take that man. He is a criminal or rebel." They took me to the authorities of Aringa, who cooperate with the Arabs against the SPLA.

In Aringa, there was an evangelist who recognized me by name, but I didn't know him. That man was called Calamin Maring. He knew me because he had visited our area and seen me in the pulpit as a preacher. I was accused of being a member of the SPLA, which I denied. "I am not a soldier. I am in the SPLA area because all my people are living in this area. My work is preaching the gospel. That is my work." Immediately, they accused me of lying. "We know you are SPLA." They took me into custody.

When Maring saw they had arrested me, he went back to the cattle camp. Throughout the night, he reported the case to the church in Turkaka. He said, "Our people want to kill him." He knew that if I was arrested by these men, I would die. When he reported that to the church, the church immediately began to pray.

Meanwhile, I was happy because I'd been escorted without any problem. I knew that death is the gateway to heaven, and I was happy about that. When those guys brought me out during the night, they wanted to shoot me down. First, they beat me severely. When they beat me, I said, "I'm ok. Just do what you like to me." The beating actually was cool in my body and the beating didn't harm me. I received very great joy. Because I knew that if I died that day, I would go directly to heaven. I would go to my Father. They came and tied a cloth around my eyes and tied my hands behind my back. I was taken with other people who were being escorted to be killed. They asked me what I wanted to tell them. And I told them that I had nothing to say. I told them, "I am happy because I am going to heaven today, I am going to see Jesus." Surprisingly, one of them, the commander who was assigned to shoot us, became afraid. I don't know what happened. I waited for the gun shot and I was not even afraid. That man in command ran back and left the other men, put the gun down and just ran away. He ran crying loudly, "We want to kill a priest, and I don't want to do that." I was just an evangelist and not a priest! When he came to the camp where they were living, he went directly to the church. He cried out to other Christians who were coming to the church. He told them to go save the man of God. I recognized there was no sound of a gun and that I had not been killed, and I said, "Why did these men leave me like this?" I was just confused. I was really prepared in my heart to go.

Then the people of the church came to rescue me. "Where are you taking me?" They told me, "You are safe, man of God" and they took me to the church. The ladies heated boiling water to put in the shower place. I took a bath. They put me on a mattress under a mosquito net and the people around me started praying, "Praise God!" In the early morning nine priests arrived at the cattle camp, speaking my name, asking for me, saying, "You are killing the pastor." When they came, the captain said, "We recognized already that man is an innocent man. He is in the church." The high deacon was saying, again, "You are killing the man of God." They said, "No, we are not killing him."

They came to the church to get me. Those nine priests were saying "Hallelujah to God." We went to the church and were worshipping. When this happened, the priests commanded the church to contribute money and clothes and even the commanders who were beating me came with a big 50 kg bag of sugar. They also came with a lot of money. After worshipping, I opened the Bible to Psalm 23. "You prepare a table in the presence of my enemies." I began to say "Hallelujah! I was preserved by the hand of the Lord." I had been ready to go to heaven, and it was a miracle for me to be alive again. They talked to the cattle people and brought my cow and calf to me while I was in the church. Those guys escorted me back to the place where I came from. They carried everything for me, and I carried only my bag, with my Bible. From the money I received, I could buy 4 cows. Now, the person who stole the cow was from Bor; I came to know him. The people said they were going to make him compensate with 6 additional cows. I told them, "No, leave that man alone. It's a chance for me to have a testimony. Don't touch him." Unfortunately the man today has become a very bad thief and I heard recently he is in the prison. People tell about the testimony, calling him, "the guy who stole the cow of the preacher." I continue to pray for him, that the Lord will change him.

I got my preaching certificate in 1994. All that time I was searching for education. You see, my education was very much interrupted by the war in Sudan. I reached Class Four in 1993 but the war destroyed our village. There were no schools running. We fled across the Nile River to the Bor area. At that time, I was able to go back to school again at the Christian Missionary Society School. When I reached Standard Six in 1997, our teachers were being recruited by the SPLM and taken to war. That ended school for me until 2000. I took care of the cattle and the garden and preached the gospel. In 2000 I began Theological Education by Extension sponsored by the Anglican Church. An American man named Mark Nickel came to our village and taught all of us evangelists. We learned about how to preach the gospel, understand visions, perform the rituals of the church, and become leaders. We learned how Christian leadership differs from leadership in the world, but we didn't have a good foundation to achieve our goals. The lessons were translated from English to Dinka and sometimes we didn't get the meaning well. At that time, I came to realize that I needed more education.

In 2002 I began to move out from my village to Kenya. I spent two years at the Kakuma Refugee Camp from 2002-4. During that time, I joined a certificate course in missions in the camp. We were taught in English about anthropology, theology, apologetics, evangelism, hermeneutics, and homiletics. Those lessons gave me the desire to be in Bible School, so that I might learn the Word of God. The school was sponsored by the School of Missions, Nairobi-Thika. Later, I spent some time at their campus in Nairobi-Thika. In 2004 I was ordained as a full priest in the Anglican Church. I moved from Nairobi and came to the bishop's house here in Eldoret. He was called the Right Rev. Bishop Benjamin Mangar Mamur, the bishop of Yirool. I talked to him about my education but he couldn't help me. Then I went to Kapsoya to stay with other families from Sudan. In that process, I came to know Pastor Jairus Mosoti. Pastor Jairus began to help me study the Certificate in Ministerial Studies course (School of Ministry, Church of God). In that process I came to know more about theology and the importance of the Word, especially the course,

Preaching the Word Today.

When I finished my CIMS course in 2006, I received my certificate, but I didn't have money to proceed for my degree. So, I went back to Southern Sudan and I was appointed as a mobilizer for the Team of Assessment in our diocese. The area of Aliab needed a bishop because we had 99 churches with only 40 priests, including me. I completed the assessment which resulted in the appointment of a bishop to the area. After completing that work, I came back to Kenya looking for education in the year 2007. I didn't have funds, but I began to pray. The Lord revealed to me in a dream, "This year you will be in Discipleship College." I went looking for the bishop's recommendation, but he didn't give it to me, because he was afraid he would be asked by the school administration for money. (By the way, he is no longer a bishop). By the mercy of God, I got $100 from a certain lady who called me to her house so I might pray for them. The name of the lady was Martha Kuir Deng Bair. After prayers, she gave me money in an envelope. I didn't suspect it was that much money. When I opened the envelope, I was amazed to see it was $100 and I came directly to Discipleship College with the money. That was the beginning of 2008, immediately after the Kenyan crisis. The college opened and I began to study.

In my Christian life, the way has not been smooth. I have faced many challenges – good things and bad things. It came to pass that I realized I did not understand the meaning of the word, "cross," but the Lord was teaching me that word. In Discipleship College, I began to get the Word from the Book and the Lord Himself taught me. When I had been in Discipleship College for some time, the college hadn't asked me about money. When I got something, I paid. If there was someone who asked me who my sponsor was, I said, "Jesus is my sponsor."

That year (2008) I really had a challenge looking for money. I went back to Southern Sudan. I found an accumulation of problems in my mother's house. I had a big problem with home affairs. My sisters ran away while we were working on dowry for them. Instead, they chose the husbands they wanted, without cows. My younger brother became very angry and wanted to kill one of the guys in my presence. But I refused. I convinced them that dowry was not required in the

Bible. Because I'm the first born, they listened to me. I told the ladies to go with their husbands free without any dowry. Miraculously my younger sister was married for only 60 cows, which were given to the family. Then, my family was coming to me and telling me that I should marry so I began the process. The family found my wife for me. They asked my approval. I said, "I'll go back to school to finish first and then I will come," but they refused because my younger brothers were getting old and wanting to marry. They couldn't marry until I did, according to our culture. So I accepted, but I told them that I would be going back to the school. Me, I didn't know my future wife because I had been outside the country. I didn't want to marry because I wanted to go back to study. They said "We have some girls around." They pointed them out to me. Aker was not looking beautiful but she was working in the church. The people said, "She is a humble person." The Holy Spirit told me that this is the one, so I began to move. I paid the dowry and the high deacon of that area prayed for us. We don't have a marriage certificate, but we have a letter from the bishop. My wife, Aker, is still at home. Aker is also the name of the white cow I gave to her mother. We now have a daughter whose name is Ayen. According to Dinka tradition, when she was conceived I was to take her to my wife's family. After the child was born, the child would be left with her family. Tradition says that when she is 12 she will come back to us. When I go at the end of this year, my wife is to come with me but the child would remain with the family. The next children will remain, however, with my wife and me. Leaving Ayen with my wife's family is sort of insurance to keep the two families together. But, I'm going to dedicate Ayen to the Lord. I will withdraw the money and give it to my in-laws and then they will let me take her with us.

After I came back to Kenya, in 2009, I got an appointment from the Sudanese congregation in Kenya as the pastor in charge of Bungoma. I planted a church there and it grew. I planted another church in Pioneer at the African Gospel Church compound. In that process, an incident occurred in 2010. I began to work with the referendum process of Sudan as secretary with the International Organization of Migration. After I finished that contract, I was appointed again as an observer by the Sudan Council of Churches. After finishing the work of the referendum, I was accused by a lady, at the instigation of people in the church I pastored who were looking for position, of having an affair with her and fathering her child. She went to the police and opened a case against me of rape. She accused me of raping her on August 28, 2010 and opened the case against me on March 13, 2011. The Kenyan police refused to accept it as a legitimate case. "If the rape is true," they asked, "why didn't she report it when it occurred?" The people of Discipleship College were in prayer with me about this case. That lady who accused me of raping her said that she was pregnant with my child. I said, "If that is true, wait for the child to be born and a DNA test will be carried out." They had no proof of such a thing, but unfortunately, the leadership of the church cooperated with her and they removed me from the church and appointed another person. Later on, they realized that what they had done was not right. Now, there is a process to seek me to join them in the ministry, but I have refused. This news reached my bishop in Australia and the bishop was looking for evidence from that church in the Sudanese community in Kenya, but there was no proof. People deny that the church dismissed me but I have a letter.

I came to realize that life in Christianity is not a smooth one. But, I am happy for everything that has happened to me and have come to realize that Satan doesn't want me to be in Discipleship College and to graduate from this school. But through the prayer of the saints, the Lord has been with me. And I'm still here in Discipleship College. Praise God! Now the church is preparing a letter of apology that will be given to the college to clear my name. Through the prayers of the community of faith, I have been greatly helped. They helped me to pray for my need for school fees. In the year 2010, I was in prayer with individuals in Discipleship College. We prayed and God miraculously moved the government of Southern Sudan to give me $1000. I see that the prayer of the Community of Faith works. The Lord has helped me in many ways through this prayer. For example, when I prayed with the Community of Faith during the above crisis, I received joy, while in the natural I didn't feel that at all. To God be the glory!

(Abraham has completed his work at Discipleship College and has returned to South Sudan.)

CARE FOR THE FISH!
Christopher Mujesia Chiveyia

Development is slow in western Kenya due to traditional beliefs, witchcraft and polygamy. Thus, in spite of the fact that Western Kenya has a climate conducive to farm production and animal rearing, many homes are devastated and people are stricken in spirit, lazy and very poor. Our family was no exception. Born to a family of eleven, I am number seven. I made my appearance on the second of September, 1966, in Shinyalu district, Shiakungu location, Solyo village.

Both my parents are illiterate. My father managed to learn English, the alphabet and a few words here and there after attending nursery school and progressing on to Standard One back in the thirties. My mother was not lucky at all for she was brought up believing that education was not necessary for women – that the woman's place was in the kitchen. She was not allowed to eat eggs, chicken or pork. It was believed that if she ate chicken, when the time came for giving birth, she wouldn't succeed in delivering the child. With my lovely parents in a state like this, I've come to believe this was the beginning of a long walk into hardship and struggles. There was not much for them. They themselves barely had enough to eat. Their story is that in fact sometimes there was nothing to eat at all. Traditionally, it was believed, that the more wives you had, or impregnated, and the more children you had, the more you proved to be a real man. As a result I have six brothers that I don't know and other sisters, who have married. Two of them tried to build in our home compound, but we did not allow them. Having struggled to bring up so many

Tea Without Sugar: Chastened for a Destiny

children, trying to put them to school with no success, my father left home to a destination unknown to his parents or to my mother or to all of us children. There were few landline phones and no cell phones. One had to walk, or if lucky, ride a bicycle eleven kilometers from our home to Kakamega town to make or receive a phone call from people working mainly in Nairobi. My father was a tailor. One of the reasons he disappeared from home was that he was indebted to many people. He took their money but did not buy the fabric for the clothes he was supposed to make. There were piles of tattered clothes, that were meant to be repaired, while he squandered the money of the owners.

At age seven I noticed how my mother took a small sharp tool called an *emboko* to weed on a maize and beans plantation. She would come back with a little maize flour to prepare *ugali* (boiled corn cake or maize porridge) with some traditional vegetables. These herbs were called *sheriezo* and were the usual greens eaten by goats.

"How does my father look?" I asked with tears rolling down my cheeks one evening. "Haven't you seen one of his photos?" my mother asked in reply, as she looked at me. Then she said, "Tomorrow, I'll take you with me to the Jakobeti home. We will do some work so that you can get books and uniform to start school." While we were working together on unplowed land, my mother revisited my previous question. "Why did you ask about your father yesterday?" "I want to see him. I want to tell him what I want. My friend's father comes every Christmas and brings them gifts." It was near Christmas time and my mother had planned for me to join Standard One the next year. We worked for two weeks and a few days at Jakobeti's home, but for me it seemed like a lifetime. The food at the Jakobeti's home was so nice. For the first time I ate tomatoes and fried meat. "When I grow up, I want to be a teacher," I said to my mother. "Good, good, very good, my son, and you will be," she encouraged me. We took turns among ourselves to go out and work with our mother. This is how we got food and books and met our educational needs. My mother worked for various teachers. We were seven brothers and three sisters. Our first born passed on before I could know him, but the rest are still alive. The stories of my brothers and sisters are a whole book in themselves.

After completing my primary education, a neighbor of ours who was working in Eldoret, let us know that my father was in Eldoret. I searched in vain to find his photo. My cousin, a son to the man who told us where my father was, was coming to Eldoret. I begged for money to accompany him there, but we could not afford to raise transport from Kakamega to Eldoret. Finally, my mother borrowed money from one of our teachers to assist me. It took some days to find my father after I arrived in Eldoret. My dad had started to sell spare parts for bicycles and to work part-time as a guard. He had plenty of excuses why he did not want me to stay in town. He told me if I stayed in town, I would start smoking and drinking. He lamented how everything was bought in town – from a matchbox to the sweet potatoes and cassava we had free at home. Even at home we had borrowed match sticks every evening. If not, we waited for a neighbor to light a fire. Then we would go with sticks to light them in order to carry the fire back to our house.

It was 1980 when I came to Eldoret. One day while walking in Langas Estate, I heard announcements about a crusade. I was curious about what a crusade was, because there was nothing like that back at home. The preaching was nice and convincing about how Jesus had given his life for us, how one can inherit the kingdom of God by being born again. When the altar call was made, I gave my life to Jesus Christ. We were many who responded. They prayed for us as a group, counseled us, told us how to walk a Christian life, assured us that we were forgiven and that we had begun a new life. They taught us how to pray, read the Bible and get to a salvation-believing church. I didn't have a Bible and I didn't know where to find a church.

But the next Sunday I found a Pentecostal Assemblies of God Church. When they asked for visitors, I testified that I had received salvation at the crusade and that was why I had come.

I stayed around with my dad for another year before I joined high school. In 1982, I tried attending classes. After a few months my mother visited us. When my mother came she took me to school and helped me enroll in Form One without money. I again say thanks to my mom. I tried attending classes, but I was away every now and then because my father did not pay school fees. My performance in Form One was so poor that I had to repeat it. When I asked my father to come to school, he came, promising to pay, but did not pay.

From 1983 to 1984 I witnessed to many students in school talking about my salvation. I preached in school assembly and I was chosen the Christian Union chairman. Our C.U. patron paid part of my school fees in Sirikwa Secondary School. Some of the people I witnessed to are pastors today. Some of them are Pastor Wycliffe Alumasi in Tarbo Town, Geoffrey Munialo, a Bible expositor on radio and a pastor in Nairobi, Pastor Ben Munialo in Chicago, Pastor Jonah Shirutsi in Pioneer, Eldoret, Pastor Phyllis Mukanda in Kitale, and Pastor David Kiprotich, a pastor and a student of Discipleship College.

After my Form Two exams in 1984 in the Kenyan Junior Secondary examinations, I remained with one paper (exam) in Kiswahili. One day, when I went back to our house in Langas where I resided with my dad, to my utter shock, I saw that my father had carried away everything from the house, leaving me with a portable "safari" bed, my two pair of shorts, one blanket, and my books. There was no stove, no money, and no note – nothing. I fell into my small bed and cried until I could cry no more. I slept for about two hours on the bed that day. I awoke around seven, visited my friends, one by one, in the estate. I ate lunch here, supper there, and went back to our house to sleep. The landlord came to the house for our 500 Kenyan shillings rent. He told me my father had arrears for some months. He did not disclose to me the number of months, in spite of my insistence. He locked me out. I spent a few days at my friends' homes, sometimes without eating at all. "What if someone goes in the night and steals my belongings?" I wondered. That day I went and sat near the plot of our house. Evening came and I stayed at the same place.

Nobody plans how to spend a night in a trench. But, the night came, and I was seated on the edge of a trench with my feet down in the trench. I felt my legs were warmer than the upper part of my body. Later I decided to lie down in the trench, convincing myself that I would know what to do later. The next thing I knew, it was morning. I opened my eyes. My body was numb. I never had a thought of danger, or "What if?" if I slept. The Bible says, "He gives sleep to those who trust in Him." I had gotten a solution for sleeping. For one week I slept in that trench. Thanks be to God it was the dry season. Sometimes, I think I could do it again! As soon as the sun rays would strike my spot, I would wake up in style, lest people would notice that that boy had slept all night in the trench. I would come out when everyone had woken up and about one hundred metres from that spot was a path crossing over the trench. By 5am people were going to work, especially at the Rivatex factory. I would rise, sit on the edge of the trench and pretend that I had gone there in the morning to bask in the sun. Then I would walk away.

"Do you know your father has another wife?" One of my father's friends asked me one morning, adding depression and confusion to my mind. He described to me how the woman looked, where they stayed near town and how I could get to them. At that time Moi Referral Hospital was just a medical center and that is where my father had moved. I went to the place, but I found that they had moved to Busia in western Kenya on the Ugandan border. One day the landlord came back, asking if I'd gotten the house rent or if my dad had come back. He listened to me and allowed me into the house, promising to help me. On entering the house, I deeply reflected on my life and all the hardships I'd gone through. There was poison for rats and chiggers in that house. After deep thoughts of rejection, feelings of loneliness and abandonment, I decided to take a mixture of that poison. I thought I would die peacefully lying on the small bed. But, I discovered that dying is not as easy as I thought. The flashes of pain in my stomach, sweating, wanting to vomit without anything to vomit out, the discomfort, painful eyes, etc., made me cry out. The landlord had put a padlock on top of ours. I had convinced him that there was nothing there except my few things. I cried out in pain and desperation. I was unconscious for some time. I had taken the poison around seven and by 9:30 the pain was terrible. It was like I was coming out of myself. I don't know how my immediate neighbors took me to a clinic at 10:00 that night. I found myself in a hospital where there were very few people. On studying the movements of the doctors and the two nurses, I discovered there were chances to leave the clinic without being seen. When the doctor came, he asked me who brought me and I did not answer. "What happened?" I did not answer. "Who will pay for your bill?" I had made up my mind to not talk. So I escaped from the clinic after a few days of treatment, knowing that I could not pay the hospital bill.

Tea Without Sugar: Chastened for a Destiny

When I went back to the house in Langas, the Good Samaritan neighbor narrated the whole story of the night they took me to the hospital. My tongue was out, they were trying to keep me from biting it, and I was having convulsions. My skin had changed and the veins on my hands had turned black. I had dark patches all over. When I recovered, I found out how to get to our landlord's place, remembering his promise to help me. I went to him courageously, asking him to give me my belongings which he had taken away while I was in the clinic. He ran a hotel in town, (New Ruare Hotel opposite Eldoret post office). He welcomed me, asking me where I had been. That same day he employed me as a watchman. My salary was Ksh 140 a month. I was so excited. I thanked God.

We agreed that if he found me sleeping, he would deduct twenty shillings every time he found me. I tried to keep alert for the first few days. He allowed me to eat only lunch in his hotel. The job was difficult. I guarded his lodgings where people could come in and leave at any time. It was exciting when I began, but later on it became so heavy and discouraging. Since the landlord lived nearby the lodgings, if a vehicle hooted for some time at the gate of the lodging, he would come out yelling at me. When he got my attention, he would finish by saying, "Your twenty shillings is gone." I was so troubled. I had a big club, like a hockey stick. I wore an overall with a blanket lining on the inside. I could not manage to stay awake all night, so I ended up with 60 Kenyan shillings per month. But I would console myself, "I'm not paying rent, I don't need a house, I have one meal a day." My landlord would sometimes sympathize with me and buy one quarter kilo of sugar to make some tea during the cold hours – especially at 3am when it was raining.

"Mzee, fungua!" (Old man, open the gate!) was one statement that drained all the joy, hope and enthusiasm from my heart. These words came from one of the clients who used to spend his nights in the lodging. After opening his room, checking him in, I went out in tears. I said, "At age 17, without a house, one meal per day, no father or mother around, no wife or children, I have nothing, dropped out from school, now I'm already old." I prayed and cried and opened my heart to God that night. I remembered the prayers of my mother for us, when she would pray. She would just talk to God telling him all that was going on. She would say, "Help these children like the vegetables without oil. Help them to appreciate themselves, not to feel inferior, not like others," and many prayers like this, often quoting Psalms 23 and finishing with the Lord's Prayer. And so I talked to God like that, too. "Am I really old? Help me to know that I still have hope, that I can be better than this." This happened several days. The lodging I guarded was at West Eldoret, between the market and the estate. I left my job at 7am, walked slowly and sleepily through town to Nandi Garden, near the Eldoret-Kapsabet bridge on the River Sosiani. I slept in Nandi Garden until afternoon. I went back to the hotel, which was near the post office, for lunch. After lunch, I would go either to the field at Town Hall or back to Nandi Garden for a nap, then straight to duty at 5:30 pm.

I guarded for about a year and eight months. While sleeping in Nandi Garden, an evangelistic team used to come between 12 noon and 2pm. I did not have time for them, since they came when I was leaving, but one of the afternoons I overslept. I awoke to nice gospel music. A brother by the name of David Omwanza played the accordion to the tune, "Oh, God is Good." Oh, how I admired the singing. I missed my lunch that day. They preached and I went forward to be prayed for. I had stopped going to church. I was confused. They invited us to their fellowship which was in the upstairs of the FIMS building. A school had rented that building, called Sisibo Secondary School (which eventually became the school grounds on which Discipleship College is now located.)

I went the following Sunday; by 8:30 am I was at the building. Sunday School children came in at around 9am. They played, ran around in the classroom until time for the main service at 10:00 or 10:30. I got interested in playing the accordion – one of my best instruments now. After a few lessons from David Omwanza, I began to play, though not perfectly. I was disturbed and burdened that there was no Sunday School teacher in the church. After several services, I volunteered to carry the accordion for David from Chepkoria House to the FIMS building every Sunday. I noticed the room we were meeting in was very dirty. I decided to do two things for the church – sweep and clean before the main service and teach the small children. I just wanted to control them so they wouldn't run around and make it dirty again. After sweeping the first day, getting some water from River Sociana, the Sunday School children came in. I made them sit down, we sang and I prayed with them.

Many Sundays came and went. I would play the accordion for the children; tell them stories from the Bible. I had asked my landlord for one of the Gideon Bibles that was in the lodging. I could also remember the stories I was taught in Sunday School back home. (From the time I was little, I was encouraged to go to Sunday School by my mother. We would go there at around 7am in the morning every Sunday). I told them about David and Goliath, Elisha and the children who were eaten by bears, Jesus and the children, and other stories. After teaching I would put the accordion in its case and wait for David to play in the main service. Later on, in the course of the year, 1985, the bishop of the fellowship came to this little church. We were about 25 to 28 members. He came at 8am, parked his bicycle and came and sat in the room where we met. I didn't know he was the bishop. I thought he was just another visitor. I came in with the children. They would come from Pioneer and from town. They now knew who was teaching the children. The parents asked me to come by and collect them. The older ones would help clean the place. The bishop stood outside waiting. Little did I know he was listening to what was going on. After dismissing the Sunday School children he asked me where I came from, if I was in school, how I started to teach the Sunday School children, and so on. He was so shocked when I told him I was a watchman. I showed him my club, my overall and my mason-like cap. I narrated my story to him, though I left out most of the details. "My father left me here, I was told he married someone else; I looked for a job and became a watchman." He asked me if I would sing the songs I sang with the children in the main service and I accepted. But when the main service began, I became nervous and trembled. David had not come to the service for a few Sundays. Before the opening prayer was finished, I looked around to see if David had come in, but he had not, so I picked up the accordion and slowly taking my watchman work tools with me, I disappeared. I then moved very fast, wondering what they would say if I was not there. I'd gotten so used to the children. In every service, I would wonder if the parents knew who cleaned this place and taught their children. I'd get discouraged but I would say. "I'm doing this for God." For about three weeks I did not come to church.

At the same time, my lunch was cut off at the hotel. I was not doing my job well. Now that I had been in the church, I would forget that I was supposed to sleep. Sometimes, a friend would invite me to lunch and I would forget to go to sleep and come late to church. Sleep was overwhelming me. After hearing my testimony, a sister by the name of Flora Bartera had invited me often to take lunch at her place. But other times for lunch I had was just a piece of toast and a cup of tea.

David had been out on a mission. Actually the reason I disappeared from church was because he had stopped coming to teach me. One day his team sang in the open air out in the garden. He was playing and singing and he asked me to come and sing with them. "Where have you been? Come and sing with us." I testified how I was born again, that I had received some peace. "Even though I'm a watchman, I have peace." I went back to church that week. As usual I swept and cleaned and taught the children. The bishop invited me to his office. He was coming to town to make Eldoret his headquarters because there David was not in Eldoret. David had been preached to by him and had become the pastor.

I started looking for a job and I was employed as a salesman with the Singer company-Amedo Centre. I was paid on a commission basis. I did well. All this time I was thinking of my siblings and my mother at home. From the money I earned, I went back and built my mother a house. From a grass house, I had progressed to a house with iron sheets. Praise God! There is help in God. I also helped two of my brothers to go on with their education.

I went to Bible School in 1990. After two years of diploma course, I came back and asked the bishop to help me to go and start a church in a place called Nandi Hills. I had a strong conviction from the Lord. I began the church with six people. The church grew to 300 members; among them were respected members of society, e.g. a district commissioner, tea factory managers, medical nurses and teachers. I admit that I was naïve in leadership. The favor was there, the resources were there, but I did not have wisdom. Wrangles began in the church with a few elderly people wanting positions of leadership and authority in the church. Out of ignorance I divided the church. Most of the members supported me. We had tried to buy a field for the church, bought instruments, etc. When I declared I was leaving, the elders took away everything the church had bought me, including kitchen utensils. I made the mistake of announcing my intentions to leave, for I gave people a period of one month to state my mistakes, to come to me if I owed them anything, to call the Bishop and state the problems they saw. After all of those who wanted leadership saw the opportunity, they went to the Bishop, convinced him that I was out to destroy the church. He believed them and wrote me an expulsion letter. I said, "NEVER AGAIN, NEVER AGAIN will I be called a pastor."

I will not forget that day because my fiancée, Faith, was visiting. We had not seen each other for a long time. She is the lady to whom I am married today. It was on a Sunday. I was leading the morning intercession with about thirty members present. The elders were aware of the Bishop's letter, so they stormed in, pulling me from the pulpit, out through the church door. There was no service that day. I stood outside; members flocked to me on hearing what had happened. They went into the church praying, some crying. They demanded to know, "Why?" "What had their pastor done?" There was no good answer except that the Bishop had written a letter that I must leave. When I went to my house, the members followed me. We sang and this was the ground-breaking of a wonderful church, but I had no peace. I prayed and asked God to allow me to do something else.

After a few months, I received a letter to go back to college (Victorious Living Ministries in Bungoma) to finish my diploma course. Someone had looked into the records and decided to sponsor me. After the course, I was employed by the same college. I held different positions in the college, including store-keeping, Dean of Students, teaching and board member.

When the college closed, I was among the two people appointed to represent the college in East Africa. We travelled extensively in Kenya, Uganda and Tanzania, opening small bible schools, translating English materials into Kiswahili, ministering in the churches of the college graduates.

When it was time to marry, it was difficult for me to be accepted by my parents-in-law. Why? Because preachers don't have money and I came from a poor family. I was nick-named "street boy," which I completely accepted. In fact, I was less than a street boy for almost 2 years. It took us six years in courtship before we got married (1991-1996).

After the work of traveling and ministering with VLM for two years (1998-2000), I felt tired. I did not enjoy sitting in an office waiting for invitations. I wanted to preach, reach out. The college had closed; I could not do what was in my heart. Disturbing dreams started to occur to me when the evening came, I literally was afraid to go to sleep. During this time, I prayed, read books, delayed to go to sleep and gazed at the roof. But no matter where I was when sleep came, there was this terrifying vision. I would find myself being pulled by a strong force through a hollow pipe-like entrance and very fast, finding Jesus on a shore of a lake or ocean. Coming from behind him, I would see him crouching, fishing. I had practiced fishing with short fishing lines in rivers at Rural. I had watched the Jesus film. So I knew his backside with his long hair. The first time I dreamed, it was a good experience up to this point. The Lord was fishing very fast, throwing the fish as if they came directly from the hooks. He seemed to fish with two lines and both hands. They fell back behind him, struggled through the sand on their way back to the ocean. Having listened to the voice of the Apostle Peter in the Jesus film and counting him to be one of the Lord's favorite disciples, I thought I should imitate Peter's voice, to address the Lord. I stood there, the Lord so busy fishing and, I with my heart trembling said, "Lord, Lord, they are going back." After I said it two times, I have no words to describe what I felt or saw as he turned to look at me. I never saw his face, for to me it was like a great fire with a voice thundering as if I were back in the hollow pipe. Very slowly but powerfully, he said, "Stop bothering me!" I spoke to him in Kiswahili so the answer came in Kiswahili also, "Usinisumbue." I woke up at this point, panting, sweating, trembling, gasping for breath, feeling like I was coming out of myself. It was terrible.

This happened for one year and several months from April 2000 to 2001. I began to share with a few people, including a bishop, whom I consider a mentor, who had come to Eldoret. After explaining the dream, he told me he had no answer but that I should continue to pray.

I made a habit of visiting Eldoret every now and then because my wife had gone to visit her sister in the USA and we had our children staying with their great grandmother in Eldoret.

There was a small church looking for a pastor (Community Fellowship Baptist Church). One of the key leaders in this fellowship had sponsored me to pay my house rent while in Nandi Hills. Later on he told me he had been following my whereabouts after he had heard of the division of the church in Nandi Hills. He heard that I often visited Eldoret and knew the bishop I came to see. Together with two other brothers they visited this bishop's office and told him that they were interested in asking me to pastor their church. The senior pastor had gone for further studies and some problems had developed in the church. I said, "No." I gave all the excuses and the vow I had made after my first church experience. This is when the bishop opened his eyes, and revisited my terrible dreams. He looked at me and said, "Chris, you are called to be a pastor. The Lord is doing his part; your part is to take care of these fish so they don't go back to the ocean." He told me to give it a trial again and encouraged me. Bishop Likavo has been such a blessing. He is the same person who advised and encouraged me during difficulties when I wanted to marry, encouraging me to persevere until I succeeded. I owe him a lot. Thank God for Bishop Likavo.

I went to Community Fellowship church, met with the pastor and elders and we shared. The congregation had gone through a lot. The founding pastor had left amidst confusion. This senior pastor had openly desired that the church would look for one they could call "the pastor" of the church. The church was about 20 to 25 members by the time I joined. They were meeting in a small structure on less than ¼ of an acre plot, but had potential people, with education and who might be termed "elite." I had never seen so many doctors in a church. There were about five doctorate holders, lecturers in Moi University, high school teachers and business men.

I had heard that Discipleship University was training ministers in Christian ministry. I joined in 2004, but raising fees was not easy. I took a few courses externally and then disappeared. Meanwhile, I gained more understanding on how to minister to these people. I had seen my leadership skills develop, and gained better ways to deal with issues in the church. The church had grown up to 130 members by the year 2006. When the senior pastor finished his studies, he came back and said we would work together and continue to help the church. I had a chance to visit my former Bishop Jonah. I made things right with him, and even taught for him in his Bible School in 2003 to 2006. I helped gather a few of us who were brought up in Christian Outreach Church and honored him in 2006 with gifts and blessed him.

In 2007 after the post election violence, I decided I needed to complete my degree course in Discipleship. From miracle to miracle, God has provided for my school fees.

When I look at the people I pastor today – some prominent people in the government, lecturers in colleges, high school teachers, a lawyer, business men—I am amazed. I have a home I call my own, a car, and the privilege to help the less fortunate in society. I can strongly say I am convinced that there is help in God. If he has done it for me, he can do it for anybody.

I am married to a beautiful lady, Faith, and we have two children, one in high school, our first-born girl, and a boy in primary school Standard Seven. Neeme and Nathaniel are a blessing to us.

Indeed there is help! God has used people who are not my relatives, not of my tribe, and it amazes me. Today my dad who left me and abandoned us lives in the house I built for my mom. I am treating him for diabetes and helping my parents. From nothing to a blessing, by the help of Jesus Christ, the hope of glory.

The church was affected after the post-election violence. Many people left, including the brother who had earlier sponsored me, the senior pastor and several other members. But God has brought in new people. He has helped me, also, to complete my degree programme at the college. I am grateful.

(Since the first edition, Chris' father has gone to be with the Lord. Chris currently serves as Dean of Students, Campus Pastor and Lecturer at Discipleship College as he pursues a Master's Degree in Bible and Theology through the African International University).

PREGNANT FOR 18 MONTHS!
Mary Nakalembe Kyalagamba

Having a son is a "must" for an African man. Because my father needed a son, even before I was the born, the fourth child of my parents, my father had taken a second wife and later he took a third. You see, all of his wives had at least two or three daughters before they had a son. Eventually, all together there were twenty-four siblings, of which sixteen have survived. Our home life was hard because each woman looked after her own. For example, at mealtime, each one would take her little flock off in a corner to feed them. I knew it was hard for my mother and me, too. I am Mary Nakalembe Kyalagamba. I was born in Seeta, Uganda near Kampala to Mr. James Kyalagamba and his first wife, Mary.

When I was growing up Seeta was a village, but now it is part of Kampala. We had a small plot of land which we tilled. Most of the responsibility for the property and children fell upon my mother. My father was a business man, buying and selling coffee for export. After that job, he worked as a personnel manager for Coca Cola. For the coffee exporting he had traveled a lot, but for Coca Cola he was working in the factory.

When I was a little girl I loved to sing, especially hymns. My mother was a Catholic, my father an Anglican. We tended to follow the Anglicans, though I was baptized a Catholic. I grew up in the time of Idi Amin. Idi Amin's goons wanted to kill my father because he had money and some of his things were confiscated. We children didn't feel anything hard, though, because we were just young and did not know what was taking place. I do remember that when Amin took over, I was beginning class one The neighbors sent someone to tell us not to go to school because Idi Amin had taken over the government. We had already gone to school, but someone came for us to take us home, because no one knew what would happen. We stayed home for almost a week, but things seemed to settle down and life continued as usual.

Seeta primary school was large – having 7 classes. I studied there from P1 to P4. I enjoyed school, especially the games. For me, the teachers were good. From P5 my parents put me in a boarding school called Matale school. At Matale, the teachers gave me the position of being the time keeper because I was always late. That helped me, because I had to ring the bell, I couldn't do it if I were not dressed. My favorite subjects were mathematics and science, and I wanted to be a doctor because when I had been taken to the hospital one time, I had admired those people who had been treating me.

I stayed in Matale school until I completed primary level. Then I went to Mukono Bishop's Secondary School. I did not board at that school. When I started Senior 2, my first child was born. It was hard for me. My dad took me back to school again after the baby was born. He wanted me to be a lawyer. So I went back and finished my O levels. My father at this point could no longer provide my school fees, so I had a friend who wanted me to tend his shop. There I met the father of the other five children that I have mothered. He was an engineering student. After my second pregnancy, I went to live with him. Like most people, we did not get legally married. He also dropped out of school, because his sister confused his mind and convinced him to go to a farm where we grew sugar cane. We were making *jaggery* from which liquor would be made. It didn't prove to be a good business.

When I was pregnant with my fourth born child, I was unable to deliver him. At 18 months of pregnancy, I was feeling desperate. My skin was like ashes and my appearance was not good. I was almost dying. I had gone to see doctors. They had told me I needed to be operated on, but then they would say I didn't have enough blood. So they would tell me to go home and eat such and such so that I would become strong enough for the operation.

About that time, a group of evangelists came from Kampala preaching the Gospel. They prayed for me. One of the women preachers had had a vision and God directed her exactly to where I was staying. This woman saw that someone had done witchcraft and put those witchcraft articles on a grave. She told me that I would see

Tea Without Sugar: Chastened for a Destiny

something after three days (they were fasting) that would confirm her words. They prayed for three days and then I delivered my baby of about four kilos in size. I never had any trouble and delivered without anesthesia.

At this point I was a staunch Catholic. Now I began to really depend on God. I had already given everything up to God because my life was so hard. When those evangelists prayed for me, they gave me hope. But, even then, I had been very stubborn. I told them, "If you want me to believe in your God, let Him deliver me from this problem. Then I will believe He is a good God."

I told the father of my children about the miracle and he praised God, because he had also expected me to die. I started going to a Pentecostal Church, but he remained a Catholic. But, he was unfaithful to me and was a drunkard so finally I felt there was no need for us to stay together. As time went by, I began to reflect on the events of that day when I had delivered my baby. On that day, I had been riding on a tractor. The driver was taking me to buy a fish. We met a black snake on the road. It passed by and fell down the other side and died, but the tractor had not hit it. At that time, I did not think anything about it, but later, I began to think it had significance, because on that very day I gave birth. Later on I came to understand that there was another woman who wanted to marry my "husband."

The father of my children and I lived together until 1992. I really don't remember any good times. We had left the farm after a few years and returned to Mukono where we rented a house. I was doing small jobs to earn a bit of money. He was doing the same, but we were not making it financially. When the landlord came to collect the house rent after many months, we were told to vacate. My husband took his things and left and I also went home with the kids. According to our custom, he should have taken responsibility for the kids, but he did not, so I took them home to my parents.

My parents were not happy at first. But my father stood by me and gradually my family accepted my presence back in the house. I took care of the children and was looking after the plot while my mom and dad had to help out with providing food for my family. I was going to church, trying to learn more about God.

There was a special time when the Holy Spirit fell on me. We were in fellowship. The Holy Spirit fell on me and I could see some things clearly. There was a woman who had put some small things in a bag under her bed in a basket. I saw them and told her, "The Lord wants you to put those things on fire, so that you can be pure." When I spoke, she admitted that the things were there, but she did not want to burn them. Someone had given her these things. She brought them and we saw them, but she wanted to give them back to the person who gave them and not burn them.

One time I prayed for someone to be healed. John and Sarah (my sister and brother-in-law) had called us to pray for a mad person and God delivered her! She came carrying many dirty things which she would move about with. When we entered the church, we immediately prayed for the woman. She was healed and she could now regain her memory. She knew how to return home and she testified that God had totally set her free. She shaved her hair and we gave her new clothes. We gave her transport and she went home. To God be the glory!

Pastor Joseph and Katherine Kagarama pastored me and discipled me. As time went on, we began to have a home fellowship in Kireka (near Kampala) at the home of John and Sarah. Gradually the group grew larger and became a church. The first pastor was Pastor Latim. I was one of his workers and when he was absent I would moderate the service and preach. When he was given another church, I began to pastor the Kireka church. This church (which has papyrus walls) is still located on the property of John and Sarah.

In 2004 Pastor Kagarama suggested that I attend Bible School, because I was the leader of the home cell groups in Seeta. We had already started the church at Kireka. After two years I finished my certificate. Then he suggested I should continue my education by enrolling in Discipleship College, Eldoret, Kenya. It was very hard for me to be so far from home, especially because I knew my precious daughter, Miriam, was dying from HIV/Aids, but I persevered and graduated in 2009.

At the present time I continue to pastor the Kireka church and am a lecturer at Seed the Faith Bible College where I received my certificate. Miriam has now passed away and I am beginning again to raise a family: her four children, the youngest of which also suffers from HIV/Aids. God is my strength for this big task.

Tea Without Sugar: Chastened for a Destiny

LIFE AFTER GENOCIDE
Janvier Nsanzumuhire

41-year old Janvier looks like a teenager in his bleach-modified blue jeans and t-shirt. But Janvier has endured many hardships to come to this place in life. He was born the second oldest in a family of seven to a Rwandan farmer and his hard-working mate. From the beginning life was difficult. His father was a drunkard and didn't care well for the family. His mother had to work very hard to provide for the children. When Janvier was 7 years old he started to school. But school fees were hard to come by. His mother tried her best to help him.

He says, "When I reached standard four my mother became sick. I stopped school for 4 months. During that time my mother's family decided to take her to their home, so my siblings and I stayed behind with our father. Life became even more difficult. My mom's sickness took a long time to heal – four years. Her family tried to take her everywhere possible to get help but she didn't get healed. Because life was such a strain on all of us, I tried to find work to do to help myself and also to assist my mother. At that time, in 1985, our family members were not born again. We were irregular church-attending Catholics. But, at 12 years of age I made a vow to God. I was in a quiet place where I could really concentrate on praying. I prayed fervently and sincerely to God asking him to heal my mom. I promised that if he healed her, I would be His servant. I made this vow without really knowing God. The idea of a vow came to me because I saw how my Mom was suffering so much. Even the doctors and witch doctors did not think she could be healed. They told our family just to take her home and wait for her to die. That was a very difficult word to hear. During that time she just slept and she weighed only 35 kilos.

Two years later some evangelists led by a man named Gaspar came to Mom's parents' home where she was staying. They asked where Turio (my mom) was. She was in her room sleeping because she couldn't walk. When they were taken to where she was, they started to tell her about Jesus Christ. They told her only a few words. The message was simple. "Turio, if you receive Jesus, he can heal you." So my mother questioned the evangelist, "Gaspar, your Jesus can heal me?" "Yes, Jesus can heal you." So my mother said, "I believe." She confessed her sins and she received Jesus. Then he prayed for her.

After praying they left, but my mother immediately showed she had great faith. She stopped every medicine because it had come from witchcraft. She told my grandmother, "From now on I will not take any medicine. I believe Jesus has healed me." My grandmother became angry because when my mother stopped drinking that medicine, she appeared to suffer very much. She had pain in every part of her body. Grandmother said, "If you stop this medicine, you will not live one week before you die. This action looks like you are making suicide." But my mother said, "I will not die. I will serve God." So, her family and I were waiting to see what would happen after that – would she be healed or would she die? One day passed, two days, three days - nothing. One week passed. Then she started to sit up in her bed. We started to wonder, "What is happening?" After two weeks she started to stand with the help of the wall. Soon she started to walk along the wall. After two months, she started to go outside to sit in the fresh air. Many people came and said, "What has happened?" Even my grandmother started wondering what it meant to be saved and to be healed because they had been waiting for her to die, not to be healed.

Another month passed. She started to go to a nearby church (Church of God) to worship. After that, I started remembering my prayer from two years before in which I promised God that I would serve him if she was healed. I started to go with her to the church, to worship God. I even sang in the choir. My mother became an evangelist. She started to go different places to testify what God had done for her. Many people liked to listen to her and her testimony. Everywhere she went, I also went. She became an intercessor. She started to teach me how to pray, also. I began to like praying. She would call me to come to her parents' house to pray. In 1991 she came back to our home. I was so happy that we had started to become a family again. But during that time our country was facing a war and we had many difficulties because of insecurity.

When mother came back home it was difficult for us to walk freely in the village because of tribal problems. I started to fear greatly concerning these problems. At this time the Hutu tribe began killing Tutsi's (my tribe) so we were very cautious about going out. The animosity had begun during colonial days because the colonizers used tribal conflict to control the people. Germans, French and Belgians were all involved.

In January 1993 my mother took me into a room privately. We started to pray. After prayer, she told me, "Janvier, my time has come to an end. It is time for me to leave." "Where do you want to go?" She said, "You will know, but you have to be strong. I have taught you to pray. You have to pray. Every problem that you have, remember God." After two months (March) she took me into a private room again and we started to pray. She laid her hands on me and prayed for me. I couldn't understand what she was doing. Why was she paying special attention to me? I couldn't understand why she singled me out.

One night, after that prayer, I came home late from work. It was very dark because we didn't have street lights. We chose to use shortcuts rather than use the main streets because there was so much danger. But there were dangers in the shortcut, too, that I didn't foresee. When I was walking I fell into a hole that was 12 meters deep. Because of my fear I had forgotten the hole which they intended for a "long-drop" toilet. When I fell inside I thought I was dying. I blacked out. I had broken ribs, an injured back and right leg. Just as I came back to my senses I remembered what the place was. Then I started to pray and ask God to save my life because I knew I couldn't get out of that hole. There was little oxygen so far down and I felt very bad. It was very dark in the hole. I tried to shout and to call people but no one could hear my voice. My voice was very small because of my injuries. As I lay there I remembered that my mother had prayed for me and laid her hands on me. After a few minutes, because the hole was near a well, I heard two people talking to each other while they stood at the well. I discovered that I knew one of them. He was standing near my hole which was on the way to his home. After finishing their conversation that man came near me but because of lack of oxygen my attempts to call him, "John, John," were barely heard. Finally he said, "yes?" "I'm Janvier," I said. "I fell into this hole; please help me to get out." He became afraid for me because he knew that hole. He called many people who came there. They tried to take me out but they failed to reach me. During that time I started to feel very ill. One of the men who came to help was one of the men I was afraid to meet because he was very dangerous. He told others to go away because he was going to help me. He put a rope around his waist and started to come down to me in the hole. It took him time but he finally reached me. He started to tie me with the rope so that the people who were above me could start to lift me out of the hole. He even helped me to go up until I reached the top. When I got oxygen I felt I was going to pass out, but after a few moments I revived a bit. I still couldn't stand or sit because my body was so broken. They phoned my family and took me to the hospital.

Because of the war the hospital was filled with many people, including soldiers. But there was no one to take care of me. The longer I stayed in the hospital the sicker I became. Because of the many sick people there were no beds. They just put me on the floor. I couldn't get someone to care for me - no doctor or nurse. I just slept alone on the floor. After one day I felt desperate because I had no medicine and the pain had became very intense. For two more days no one had come to see me and the suffering had become unbearable. That Friday I couldn't sleep or do anything. Around 6 pm I covered myself with my bed sheet over my head. I started to cry and prayed to God. "Please take me to heaven because I'm suffering too much. And nobody wants to help me. So, please, please take me home," I cried. During all that time I'd not been able to sleep but after praying and crying I slept. I dreamt. In that dream I saw many doctors and nurses come around me where I was lying on the floor. One was very tall. I couldn't see his face but I knew he was the leader of the group. They had much medical equipment. So when I saw them, I became happy. In all that time no one had come to see me – so to see someone there to care for me made me very happy. Those doctors started to touch me and work on me. One gave me an injection. They helped me in every way possible. The dream lasted for two hours. After they had helped me, the leader said to me, "You are healed." With that, they left. At that moment I woke up. When I woke up my pain was even more than before. But I realized that it was Jesus who had touched me and I trusted He was healing me. On Saturday morning doctors from the hospital finally came. They told me, "What are you doing here?" I wondered about that question. I said, "I'm sick. I'm suffering." One of them said, "Are you really? Wait for me." I thought he would come to give me medicine, but he left me, prepared a paper, and told me to go home. I was wondering why. I started to cry, "Why has this happened to me?" Then I remembered the dream so I said, "Thank you. You have touched me, Lord." My family tried to put me in a car and bring me back home. My mother continued to pray for me. After one month, without medicine or anything I slowly started to learn how to walk. My leg had been broken in two places. After two more months I went back to my job.

Slowly the genocide was starting. People were afraid. One night in July, 1993, after 4 months, again I was returning from my job. When I was on the way, I discovered many people were surrounding me. I realized that my life was in danger. They had weapons. I couldn't run. I couldn't do anything. One of them said to me, "Do you have money?" I said, "No, I don't have any." Whatever I said I would probably die. One put a knife to my stomach and said, "Now I'm going to kill you." It was possible, I knew. But, during that time I prayed to God, "Help me and receive my spirit." I was so afraid, my mind "went." I was waiting for the man to put the knife into my stomach to finish me. When my mind went, a voice came to me. A heavy voice shouted to me, "Janvier, now, run!" My mind was not alert so I don't know how I made my way between those people. I discovered I was running and people were running behind me. How I made a path between them I don't know. I ran faster than they and hid in the bush and they couldn't find me so they left. I realized someone was calling to me, "Janvier, it's me who saved you because I have plans for you." I said, "Thank you, Lord!" Because I couldn't sleep in that bush, I prayed and then went back home using the same way I had come. My mom said, "Fear not because God has a plan and He is with you."

In February, 1994, my grandmother became very sick so my mother went there to help her for all of February and March. But later in the same month she came home and called me. We sat together in the room and prayed, and after praying she told me, "Janvier, as I told you, my time is coming to leave. Please take care of your brothers." So I asked her, "What are you saying?" "Even I don't know," she answered, "but I have finished my work in this world. I don't know exactly the time but what I know is that I don't have much time left in this world." I didn't take her words seriously. After that she prayed for me again. She took her Bible and gave it to me. "In this Bible you will find every answer for your problems. If you get problems pray and read the Bible." After that she went back to her parents' home to help her mother. I stayed behind because I had the responsibility to care for the others since my father was still drinking. That was the last time I saw my mother.

In April genocide began in full force. They killed whole families including my mother, my two sisters, my brothers, and everyone who was with my mother - about 50 people. They destroyed their houses so I couldn't find them again. I remained with my father, brother, and two sisters. It was difficult at that time. We remained hidden in our house. They had started to kill our neighbors. Some of them came to us, "Ok, we will kill you," but also they brought food for us. They said, "After you eat we will come to kill you." We were just waiting to die. But, God was doing miracles for us because some soldiers were surrounding that place from the UN. RPF soldiers had taken over our place – these were the rebels – Rwandan Patrol Force – but they were mixed – both Tutsi and Hutu's. They took us to the UN control place until the genocide stopped.

God has helped me so many times. After the genocide ended in July, 1994, life remained difficult because we had lost many members of our family. We who were left started to take responsibility for ourselves. I was the one who was responsible for my family because my father was now old and unable to lead. My older brother joined the military, so I was left to take care of the rest. I was 30 years old. I tried to find something to do—anything. During that time was the time when God was calling me to enter the ministry but it took me time to accept the call. You remember, I'd taken a vow to serve the Lord. But now I felt I needed to find something to do to take care of my family. So when God called me, I refused. In 1995 I had a good job but the Lord said to me, "Now is the time for you to serve me." I refused. I remember the job I had at that time. We were making shoes in a cooperative setting. However, I lost the job without being given any reason. I knew God was doing something. But I found another job. They promised me that it was a better job than the first one. They told me to come to start on Monday. But when I arrived they informed me someone else had taken my place. I discovered it was God who blocked that job also.

In September of 1995 God called me again, "Janvier, I need you in my ministry." I explained to God why I couldn't do it. "I need to take care of my family!" God told me, "I need you." At that same time I had a very beautiful room with a closet. I left home to visit some people one night. That night a fire burnt everything I had in my room – bed, mattress, closet, everything. I don't know where the fire came from. But the fire didn't touch my father or sister's rooms. When I came back home in the morning, I saw that everything had been burnt. My father was taken to the police station because he was a drunk. They thought he was the cause of the fire. But he was not. When I entered my room, I sat down and prayed. A voice came to me, "I need you in the ministry." At that time, I surrendered all and said, "I'm coming." I took time for prayer and fasting. Then I went to the Church of God. When I entered, no one noticed me because I was small. But, I saw what God wanted me to do. During that time people came to our place because they had no place to run to. There were both Hutus and Tutsi's together in the church. Because of the tribal hatred there was not a good spirit in the church. These survivors of the genocide, both the Hutus and Tutsi's were angry, but people were hiding it in their hearts. Spiritually it was not a good situation. When I entered into the church, I asked God, "What can I do for this?" The Holy Spirit told me to start a prayer room. When I started that prayer meeting many refused to come but some came. I had permission, however, from the leaders of the church. So, we started to pray, and people started to be healed in their hearts and started to confess. Slowly God helped us to grow that prayer room. Even people from other churches started to join us. People started to ask one another for forgiveness. From that prayer room the whole church was influenced. They started to have joy, to visit each other. I discovered that was why God had called me.

In 1997 because of the impact of the prayer room, the leaders decided to take me as a leader, but I think it was God who did it. It became difficult for me because some people thought I was too young, but God fought for me. I thank God for that because I saw his hand. It was not easy. And also God took care of my family during that time even without my having a job.

In January 2000 I got money to marry. In August I was chosen to be the pastor of a church. In October our first child was born. I didn't finish my studies because of the problems in our country, but I prayed to God to open the door for continued studies. I had finished only 4th grade of primary school. But, I got no answer. In 2003 a great problem came in the church. I needed to take a stand. Taking that stand cost me dearly. As I stood for integrity, I found myself being charged in court. But the Lord intervened and I was freed. However it caused a painful split in the church. Through that I learned that I must always stand for the truth, though taking that stand would mean great trouble for me.

We began a new church that now exists. I thank God because he has defended us. We remained free to worship God and the resultant church is better than the first one. The building for that new church was a miracle of God's grace. After we started the new church we were struggling with renting a place. The church would grow but because we were renting they often needed the facilities and when we moved people would leave. So we went to rent a room of a school. The room was in a hidden place, not easy to reach. By now, we remained with only a few people. But, later the school said they needed the place. We discovered we had a big problem because we had no other place to worship God. We started to fast and pray. We saw another nearby building which was owned by the same person. He decided to give us one room where we continued to worship, but before we went there, I took time for prayer. I went to their office and started to speak to the wife of the head man. I asked her if they could sell that place. She laughed at me so much. Then she looked at me from my feet to my head and laughed more. "Janvier, you want to buy this place? Tell me, if we are willing to sell it, if you have 1 million dollars we can give it to you," and she laughed some more. I left that office, went to my room and prayed. The following day I went back again and met with her husband. God gave me favor with that man. He told me he loved me like a son. So I asked him if they could sell that place. He didn't laugh at me. He said, "If you have 500 million francs (about $833,333) you can buy it." After that my prayer group started to pray for that amount. We now had a new bishop. We brought the burden to him. He brought it to the leaders and they approved a loan from World Missions, so miraculously we were able to buy the place.

In 2008 I reminded God I needed to continue my studies. As a pastor I needed to develop myself. It had been many years since I finished standard 4 but then I began to finish primary school through an adult education course, which I finished in 2009. After that I began to prepare to complete secondary school. But at that time my bishop decided to send me to Discipleship College. Meanwhile I continued to work on my secondary school studies until the end of 2010. In 2011, I entered the Certificate of Ministerial Studies at Discipleship College. After that I continued to study for a diploma which I finished in April, 2015. My goal is to continue to finish a degree.

I have seen the hand of the Lord and I have determined to serve him all of my life. I now have a wife and 3 children, two boys and one girl. I am preparing to return to Rwanda to serve the church in whatever way He wants.

LISTEN TO THE SMALL BOY
Davis M. Gatua

Some people grew wheat in Muranga'a, Central Province, where I was born on December 27, 1966, but my family didn't. Consequently, my family would follow behind the harvesters like Ruth in the Bible, collecting the fallen kernels, hoping to have enough for *chapatis* (flat wheat bread) at least at Christmas-time. I was the fourth born of ten children to Daniel and Ann. My father was a peasant, a small-scale farmer. My mother was a housewife who used to help my father in the *shamba* (field) work. Her main duties were concentrated in the home, caring for the children and my father. During that time, as little children, we lived in a very humble manner. Our house was two rooms, with thatched roof and mud walls. We used to sleep on the floor on sheep skins and sometimes when we harvested the wheat, the straw was used as a cushion between the sheep skins and the floor. Mainly, we ate *githeri* (boiled maize and beans) with *ugali* (ground, boiled maize) and sometimes boiled potatoes. It was only during Christmas that we would eat *chapatis*, made from wheat which we had ground ourselves.

My family worshipped in a small village Full Gospel Church. Some missionaries came from Finland, named John and Maureen Walker. We little children were inquisitive about the *Wazungu* (Europeans, white people). We wanted to touch them to see if we could believe in them. There was a belief that if you touched them, you would become brilliant like them. Their message was from John 3:16, that God so loved the world that whosoever believeth in Him may have eternal life – even the children! We were many children who responded to this call. After this, the Walkers kept on coming for follow-up. They gave us some books to read and some small Bibles and even clothes. This encouraged us to remain in the church.

Even in primary school I shared the Gospel many times with the other children. We had been taught in the church how to share our testimony. I kept on doing it even in the School Assembly, before the whole student body. I received respect because I was a *prefect* (class leader). In the process, the teachers came to discover that I had a message which I could tell the children in relation to the change of behavior which came about through my belief in the Word of God. The teacher would stand by with a cane, making them sit down to listen to this small boy, because many of the children were much older than me.

For clothes, we depended on what we were given by *Wazungu*. When our clothes got torn, my father's long trousers which were worn out on the legs, were cut off and given to me to wear. These large shorts were held up by suspenders. My first time to wear shoes was when I was in Form Two. I was given shoes by a pastor who used to visit our school. He saw me preaching without shoes and he blessed me not only with shoes, but also with a blazer. Just before this time, we would go and collect some old, torn shoes from the garbage dump. We might find one shoe from one pair and one from another. Before joining secondary school, my father, who was a drunkard (my mother was a drunkard, too) used to force me and other children to work on our shamba even on Sundays, picking pyrethrum (grain used in making insecticides). We would pick this so as to get some money for the family. Every week, we would go to school two days and we would work in the *shamba* (field/garden plot) the rest of the days. Therefore, all my ten brothers and sisters dropped out of school, apart from me.

In short, I'm the only person in my father's family who joined secondary school. My father did not like that we went to school because of the school fees. To him it was an unnecessary burden. After I finished primary school, having passed my examination, I approached my pastor and told him my desire to go on with my education. He told the church and the church gave an offering to support me. He came to my father's house with some money from the church and persuaded my father to add some money to it so that I could go to school. My father insisted that he did not have money and this prompted me to go to my uncle who agreed to pay my school fees and buy my uniform. The church took care of the rest (the tuition). It was hard for me to complete the school because my father was against it, all of my brothers and sisters were at home, and nobody could assist me. But in secondary school, I was given a bursary because I was performing well in school.

With this extra help, I was able to complete Form Four. In fact, in Form Four I was the best student in Christian Religious Education in our district. I was given a reward which included a bed cover, two shirts, and a dictionary. This money helped me to join Form Five because in Form Five we were supposed to pay 2,400 Kenyan shillings to begin our studies. The rest of the money the District Education Officer paid for me. In order to pay the remainder of my fees for Form Five and Six, I borrowed money from my uncle, which I was to refund after completing my schooling.

Soon after Form Six I was employed in the same school by the Board of Governors as a teacher. My first salary was 1,400 shillings which I used to pay my debt to my uncle and also paid my father's *shamba* debt. The remaining money I used to help my father and mother with the young children. I was able to also save some. After two years I used the money I had saved to join Meru Teacher's College, for which I paid 5,700 ksh for the whole course.

In 1998 God paved a way for me to join Discipleship College to study through Lee University*. This was a big opening for me. Pastor Simon Ben of Molo told me about the college. Bishop Musa Njugana, whom I had told about my desire to study, also told me about this school. I requested Simon Ben to bring me to Eldoret, which he did and I met the director, Gordon Bloodworth for the first time. He told me to go and bring all the required documents. When I started, I could not stay on the campus, but I could study from home through external studies. I would come for consultation with Gordon and Neil Lawrence and his wife, Jennifer. I must say with a lot of humility and respect, that I owe these three lecturers lots of thanks. They kept on encouraging me and motivating me to work hard. They enabled me with their scholarly advice to finish my studies together with the on-campus students. I was the only student who was studying from home at that time who was able to graduate with the first group of graduates. During this time my younger brother finished Form Four. I was not able to take him to college because I carried heavy responsibilities. I only took him for a driving course and computer studies at the certificate level. Later, he got married, so I helped him find a place to work, where he is still working to date. The reason I could not help him was that I was taking care of my elderly parents, my own family (we had 2 children by then), and 2 foster children. In addition, my other brothers and sisters would often come to me for help, as I was the only one who was employed. The foster children were orphans who decided to stay with me after the death of their parents. As a pastor I had buried their parents who had died of HIV/Aids. The children felt comfortable with me. One of them finished her Form Four exam last year and scored an A. I'm proud of her and will take her to university. The other is still in Form Two.

After my graduation from Discipleship College in 2001, I managed to get a teaching job in secondary school in which I taught for two years. I applied for a master's degree through the University of Manchester. I was admitted and they said they would give me a scholarship after I had begun my studies with them, but I didn't have the money to go there. Then I enrolled for a masters' degree in Egerton University. I was to pay for myself all the school fees and research stipend. Because of financial restraints, the course took me four years to finish instead of two.

After my masters' in 2008, I also enrolled for PhD studies in Psychological Counseling at the same university. I am trusting God that He will provide for my fees and research money. I have finished my course work and defended my proposal and right now am working on the collections. Then I will seek the dispatch permit which will allow me to carry out the field study. My research topic is Behavior Modification among the Youth.*

While I was in my masters' course, my father who lived in Molo was attacked, beaten up, and after two months, he died. This was in 2007, during the tribal clashes. In 2008 the post-election violence struck again. My mother was evicted from her home, all her property was stolen, and her house was burned down. All of my father's children who were living there came to my house for safety. My mother was staying with me, too. After some time, our second last born decided to go and check what was happening back at home. He was caught, beaten up, and one of his eyes was gouged out with an arrow. On hearing this news, my mother was over-whelmed with fear and she became extremely depressed. I took her to the hospital, together with my brother. After a short while, my mother died of stress. Since then, I've been taking care of that brother of mine. I managed to share my belongings with my brother, whose possessions were destroyed. I took the children to school, as we were waiting for peace to be restored at home. As for now, they went back home, but they are living in a shopping center because there is no structure at home. I help them to pay the rent as they farm on my father's *shamba*.

I have organized a group in my place to help widows, orphans and single mothers. I have also organized a group for the disabled of which I am the patron. I'm hoping to be able to provide wheel chairs and other mobility aids. I also have a passion to work with children. I get troubled about how to enhance good governance and leadership in the country and in the church. I take much of my time training the local leaders and church leaders, in particular, on the importance of peace, reconciliation, and justice for all. My desire is to transform many lives through the Word of God and where possible, to author books, especially Christian literature, leadership books, and magazines. I have formulated my vision as follows, "To be an exemplary agent of change that mitigates human suffering by offering sustainable empowerment programmes." It is a big vision, but I have a big God.

My desire is to develop the small plot we are buying for the church I pastor. My prayer is that it will house not only the church, but a two-room center for the children which will be a pre- school/child care center. I desire that there will be a clinic where people can be cared for compassionately. I have seen so many women, in particular, who are afraid to go to get HIV/Aids testing. Actually, they have watched their husbands die, and know that they also have the disease, but because health workers often stigmatize and frustrate them, they are reluctant to go to get the health care that could prolong their lives. I want to help them.

*After finishing his doctorate at Edgerton University, Gatua now teaches at Kenyatta University in Nairobi.

SOAP IS ENOUGH!

Jairus Mosoti

Trees were so precious in Bomabacho village, West Mugirango in the Nyamira District, Kisii, that if my family wanted to borrow a tree to cut for firewood, and people knew we had not planted one, we would not be given a tree. The population was close to 6,000 people, but there was not even a market. Bombacho was just a group of people who were growing coffee and tea as cash crops, plus maize, beans and millet for our own use. Each family raised chickens and cattle and each family must have trees.

In the beginning, when my father was at home, life was nice. Everything was going on well because my father really took good care of us. I felt like we lacked nothing until 1968 when my father suddenly disappeared and was nowhere to be found. When my father left, we didn't know where to look. We went to his place of work in Kericho at a tea plantation. His neighbors and brothers told us they saw him in a certain place. Others would tell us that they had news of him, so we would sell something, and give them money to go find him, but no one did. Sometimes they used the money to benefit themselves. After that, all our cows were stolen and our chickens were killed. Some people would sharpen a stick and put it in the behind of the chicken so that it would die slowly. They wanted my mother to go away so they could take the land. They wanted to accuse her for my father's disappearance. From that time we became very poor. If you have no chickens, cows or goats, you have no money. My mother, who had eight children, started drinking. We didn't have anyone to take us to school, so my brothers and sisters had to drop out. We were so poor, I didn't even have shoes until I was about 20. We didn't have sugar. I could not even have identified sugar because we didn't have it at home. I could only taste sugar in chai or porridge at the neighbors. It was the same with cooking oil. Mother boiled vegetables in water only, without oil, with a little salt added.

As I grew, approaching the age of 12, I was no longer allowed to sleep in mother's house because I was now circumcised, so I moved to my uncle's children's house. Every morning I had to make sure I swept the house and made it clean or I wouldn't be allowed back in the evening. I really wanted to have my own house. Our environment was strongly Catholic and I was very religious. I believed God could hear and I believed He would give me a house. So I started planting beans in our shamba, from which I hoped to raise enough money to build a small house. I accomplished that, and soon was able to move to my own house where I did not need to bother about the neighbors. From that point on I was only thinking about going to school. I had not attended school at all, but I had always dreamed of going at least from primary grades through Form Four of secondary school. My first step towards attending school was working toward buying a school uniform. The school uniform was the biggest expense in going to school. However, it would be several years before that goal would be realized.

I had other ways to make money. I planted trees and worked in people's fields to raise money but sometimes my uncles would make me take care of their cows from morning to evening. Of course, they did not pay me, because I was their sister's child. One time I remember that I was really thinking about school when I saw my cousins coming from school. They were my age-mates. They were doing homework, talking English, reading and writing, but I could only watch them. I really desired to read and write on my own. My special motivation to learn to write was envy of their writing love letters. I wanted to write one and they encouraged me, but how could I tell them I couldn't read or write?

One time I wanted to write a letter to my uncle to ask for money to go to school. The person who wrote the letter for me, abused my uncle in the letter. Of course, I didn't know what he had written. I couldn't read. In naive trust, I delivered the letter. My uncle came looking for me. Did you write this letter? I said, "Yes." I was shocked when he said to my mother, "Now, you see, your son abusing me." I said, "I just wrote to ask you for money." "It says nothing about money," he replied. From that time on I didn't want anyone to write letters for me. I needed to go to school for myself. No one pushed me to go to school. I really wanted to go. But, I needed to raise money for that uniform. School fees weren't much – only 5 shillings a year. With one shilling you could go to a hotel, get a cup of tea with bread and get change. I remember once having a big two shillings coin. With that I could go and eat with friends and come back with change!

No matter how hard I tried, I didn't manage to raise enough for my uniform; I felt very discouraged, and began to think that I couldn't make it in life. One of my uncles used to tell me, "Your father is not here, your elder brother has also disappeared, the second has become a thug, your mother is a drunkard – you just work in the fields, take care of the cows." I nearly bought the idea, but I still wanted to go to school. I thought, "If I had the Form Four exam, I could pass it." I was determined to go to school. There was a primary school teacher in our area, named John. I would hear him shouting, "A, B, C, D." I listened and soon I could say A to Z but could not write. Then I would hear him say, "1 + 1 = 2, 2 + 2 = 4." I would practice saying those wonderful things while I watched the cows. At every opportunity, I would bring the cows near the school so that I could listen. But, if my uncle caught me he would make we go to another side. I loved it if the cows strayed into the school yard because I could say I was at school!

The vision to go to school never went away. I discovered that when you have a vision that God is leading you towards, it won't disappear. Because Form Four was such a big goal, I prayed, "Don't let me ever go beyond that." I was afraid that if I said I wanted to go to University, God might say, "That is too far." I knew, for example, if I asked most people for a tin of beans, they would give me a quarter of a tin, so I thought that if I asked God for what I really wanted, it might be too much. Even Form Four was a big dream because there was Form Two which was actually a great accomplishment, and comparable to Form Four now. You could teach or get a job after finishing Form Two. So I was saying Form Four, but thinking God might allow me to go at least to Form Two!

Life continued like this until I was 17. I remember my mother saying that wonderful year, "Will you go to school when they open?" I said, "Yes." We went to the market and bought a uniform for the first time and with 5 shillings we paid my tuition, but, even then many people discouraged me. "How can you go to school with small children? You are a big boy?" I said, "I only want to go as far as Form Four." When I was given books at school and a pen, I thought, "I am in school and I really want to go all the way to Form Four." When they said, "one," I wanted to go to a hundred. Ten wasn't enough; I wanted to go to 11. I asked the teacher how I could get beyond 10. He told me I could repeat the numbers 1-9 beside the 1. That was easy. I had started only first grade, but I already knew much of it from listening outside that school. The first term I was able to read and write from 1 to 100 because I knew the sounds; I only needed to see them. Today I still learn by listening.

We didn't have soap at home, so I took a bath only with water and went to school. I was Position One in my class every time, but the teachers would say when I stood up to receive my recognition, that my skin was so grey below my shorts, you could write on it. One time we had an exam for three or four schools, and I was number one. A teacher remarked, "Jairus got the highest marks but I think he needs more water and soap." I said, "Soap." I remember that after that day one of my teachers brought me a bar of soap. From that day my life changed. When I washed with soap, I was as clean as anybody else. I didn't apply oil to my skin until after my wife insisted on it. It seems to me that God gave me grace, so that for me, soap was enough.

I continued until Class Seven and passed the first time. I had skipped two grades, but was already 21 by the time I finished primary school. At that time there was no Class Eight. One went directly from Class Seven to Form One. However, I didn't manage to go to Form One. I was assigned to a school in Mangu district in Western Province but I didn't even know where that was. We heard stories about how dangerous it was to go to Nairobi and I would have to go to Nairobi to reach Mangu. Most people thought a person would get lost going so far. Added to the distance was the high cost. The school fees were 2400 ksh per year at the secondary school. Determined to continue, I went to ask my relatives and friends to help until one man encouraged me, saying, "I will help you go to Mangu and see." But that very day he took my certificate and took his own son to school with my certificate. Then he encouraged me to repeat Class Seven. I didn't know I could begin secondary school at a later date. I thought I had missed my chance and had to repeat Class Seven. So I did. However, I didn't attend class much. I was working to get the money for secondary school. I enrolled for the exam and went to work in people's fields, building sites, etc., to raise money. When exams rolled around, I had a B and I was admitted to two schools, but I still could not manage to raise school fees. Help, however, came from an unexpected source. One of the youth leaders in the Catholic Church who was a teacher and had completed Form Six took an interest in me. He asked me if I was interested in education. Interested? Of course, I was. At that time I only had 200 shillings, but he allowed me to stay in his house on the school compound and I began to attend school. As long as he was teaching there, I could stay in school and my mother would struggle to pay for my school fees. I didn't begin until second term and unfortunately, towards the end of third term he went to college. The head master then kicked me out of school because of an unpaid balance of 1200 ksh. I picked up my mattress and went home to work at various places. I soon raised the amount needed, but I didn't go back to the same school, because if I went back the money would all go for the previous term. At the new school students were paying 1800 per year for Form Two. I paid 1200 for one and a half terms. That time I actually managed to stay for two terms. I was again kicked out of school because I could not raise the extra 600 shillings. I went home, stayed with my mother, and worked again to raise money to join Form Three. I didn't have any textbooks, but the students who had texts lent them to me. I would read day and night while I had that book; I had to go beyond where they were because I never knew when I'd get a chance to look at that book again. When I came back to school, they were so impressed that I was not behind them that they asked, "How did you do this?" I did end up dropping math, however, because I didn't have a textbook and had heard so few explanations in class.

Finally, I went to Kericho to study. That day I had a suit and a tie on like I was going to look for employment. In fact, one *Mazungu* official in the school mistook me for a Mister Kinyanjui. I didn't know who he was, but the school official seemed to think he knew me. He smiled, "Welcome!" Then he gave me a building plan. "Ok, we took your quotation, though it was higher." He told me to sign. We went to the office and he gave me 50,000 ksh to begin the work according to the construction plans. What was I to do? "Do I run away?" I asked myself. I decided to get help. I went to a friend who was a mason. This man agreed to build the needed structure, and so it came about that I posed as the construction engineer of what turned out to be a very nice secondary school on the tea estate. Mr. Kinyanjui never showed up and I never went back to the office of that *Mazungu*. I had asked the mason, "How much will it cost to do this kind of building?" He gave the price and I did not bargain. I took him to the site and he began the work. When he started calling the engineer to inspect, they said he had done an excellent job. They said to me, "Yes, you are the right one for the job!" When the roof was on, I told him to give all the responsibility to the mason. I took money from the 50,000 ksh for my Form Four registration money and term I of Form Three, plus, I bought a cow. I talked with the headmaster, who also let me register for Form Four exams, though I was still in Form Three. I never went to that building again. Every time I was there I would feel afraid, but the building was nice. I did not want anyone in the family to know that I had done this. They could betray me as one who posed as an engineer. A few people who knew me, saw me at the school, but I just kept quiet and they didn't say anything. They only saw that I came from school. They did not know how I managed it. My mother also helped, sometimes giving me pocket money from the sale of coffee.

From then on, I stayed in school. I kept the cow at home for milk, which my brother would sell to buy whatever he needed. I was proud that I now could provide for my brothers. Eventually, two of the calves of this cow were used to pay my dowry. You see, while I was at school, I was also thinking of marriage. I didn't want to borrow money to pay a dowry; I wanted my own cows.

Those two terms I didn't do in Form Four put me out of school again, but I had registered the year before for the exams. I could go on working on our own fields and for others until I had a balance of 1250 ksh. By the time the exam results were out, I had raised the balance. I hadn't received any paper because I had not cleared the balance, but because I had performed better than the other students, the school officials were happy to see me. I didn't know what I had attained, until the headmaster said to me, "Jairus, you have come! You are the last person to come. You really worked hard to pay your school fees and you have performed well." I had reached Division III which was equivalent to university entrance. "We are not going to charge you for the balance." I was amazed. I had the money in my pocket, so I thought, "I'm rich now." With that money, I built my own big house. It was a grass-thatched house, which until now still stands but has an iron roof. I already had a cow. I was now ready for marriage.

However, I didn't marry. I committed myself in the Catholic Church to become a priest. I thought that was my way. In the priesthood, we were to take a "line," so I said that I wanted to be a teacher. I started attending classes for the priesthood at the age of 28. After some time I was employed as a teacher. I applied at a Catholic Teacher's college, however, by that time I had received the Lord, and that would present new problems.

There was a priest named Father Queen from the US, who took special interest in our group of young people. He would give us money as a reward for reading. For instance, he gave us 500 shillings to read about salvation. After we had finished reading the book, he would give us the money and say, "Now go on reading with understanding." He would ask us to defend the book against the opposing view which he taught. We would say, "Salvation is now." He would say, "Salvation is in the future." Later he would ask, "Now are you saved?" I replied, "I have received Jesus Christ as my Lord and Savior but I don't have that assurance." He would ask, "Will you get to heaven if you die today?" Then he said, "You must know you are saved and going to heaven." After we received the Lord he gave us another book about the Holy Spirit. He gave us 500 shillings more. After we had defended about the Holy Spirit, he asked, "Have you received the Holy Spirit?" He challenged us by saying, "The Holy Spirit was only for the twelve disciples." We replied that there were 120 who were filled at the beginning – then there were 3000, people from other nations. "Are you filled? he would ask. We would answer, "We haven't had that experience. We don't know." But I thought, in the Catholic Church, confirmation is when you receive the Holy Spirit, so I said, "Yes, I received it, because Bishop touched me and said,

'Receive the Holy Spirit.'" He said, "It is not given by the bishop – it is given by Christ, and it can be received anywhere. Go home, look for your place and receive the Holy Spirit." So I went home and that is how I received the Holy Spirit.

The event that made our group not finish college was receiving the Holy Spirit. Father Queen took us to private places where he would show us films. He told us he got saved when he was 20, while he was in the seminary and he was taught on how to stay saved, be Holy Spirit-filled, and to stay in the church in order to change the Catholic Church from within. He told us to stay within the church, too, to bring change but cautioned us that we wouldn't be able to stay long. The problem we had was that we had a Bible study in which we read the whole Bible, and anything the Bible said, we were convinced we must do it. When we read about images, we burned things like rosaries in the presence of church elders and people who didn't believe. This was reported to the bishop. From that moment on we were in trouble. I wasn't the leader of the group, but somehow my name was mentioned all the time. Sometimes I'd say I wasn't going to the prayer meeting so that we could stay in the room, three of us, and pray. During the mass the only thing we could say was, "In the name of the Father, Son and Holy Spirit." When other prayers were sung, we'd pray in the tune but would not pray to Mary. We didn't realize that the elders had heard us. They came behind us and listened. One of the elders tape-recorded our praying and we were taken to the priests' house and they said, "We have found out that you are no longer Catholics and you cannot be priests in the Catholic Church." I was the youth coordinator in our diocese. We debated, "What are we going to do?" We decided not to attend mass often and we scattered everywhere. We convinced ourselves to "Just pray in your spirit. Keep quiet. They see your mouth moving, but they don't know what you are saying." But, the youth did not keep silent. One day we had a diocese youth meeting. In that meeting, we said, "Friday is the day of the Holy Spirit. Keep quiet. The Lord will fill you. He is the baptizer so when you go to be baptized you just keep quiet. Then, Jesus will fill you. So, first let us pray, then keep quiet, and wait for God to fill us." One thing amazed us – everyone kept quiet. Then something began to happen in the front, people were shouting and falling. We did not know what to do. Things had gotten out of hand. We felt like running out of the meeting. One priest stood there and he was trying to say, "Quiet, quiet," but the noise just went higher. What had happened? We were about ten spirit-filled priests in training. We stopped, but these people were not stopping. Father Queen came in with other priests. They said, "What is happening? These people are crazy. Jairus is leading them. He goes with Alegio Maria (a cultic religion of Mary that came from the Luos to Kisii)." Then I was afraid I would lose my college, that I would lose everything. I was trying to make it secret, but it was never secret. These people were shouting.

It was time to go to class. People were praying and making all kinds of noise. Because the Bishop had come, I didn't want to be seen participating in anything. I tried to send my brothers to stop it. Nobody went. When Father Queen came I had sneaked out and gone to class. The bishop said to him, "You dog! Your dogs are barking over there – go and stop them." "Father, what do you want me to do?" "Don't come near me," he replied. "Look at what is happening there." Father Queen said to the bishop, "If you want this to stop, call Jairus. He did not make them to do this but I know he can stop them." Father Queen said to me, "Come." The bishop said, "What is this? How do we know? We will ask them." I stood up and said "Amen. Hallelujah." Everybody kept quiet. Then I sneaked out.

I really wanted to keep my college, but I also didn't really want to be a priest. I thought in my last year of university I could marry. When we were in the priest house, the priests would send us to find some women, take them food, and letters, or we would even take the priest, and guard the car while he would go to the women's homes. I didn't want this. I wanted only one wife.

When the people stopped praying, the Bishop said to one man, "Stephen, why were you making a noise?" The man would say, "When I went to pray, Jesus appeared to me. And he showed me -- he told me it's wrong to look for women for priests." So from now on we would not do this. The bishop would ask another. He would get another testimony. The bishop said, "Now, Jairus see what you have done." I replied, "I've not told them to do this."

He decided to prepare a rally to shame us in front of everyone because we made people cry. They brought in all the elders and the parish counsel. They sat in the front with their cigarettes, etc. They said they would make us ashamed because when we preached people would fall down. They brought everyone they thought was a real Catholic to sit at the front. I was told to preach. The Bishop said, "Now, I want to prove to everyone that those dogs are not real. I have put the dogs at the back." We told them to pray and intercede. Two of us, who were thought to be leaders, were asked to preach and pray for people, The Bishop thought our magic wouldn't work that day.

For the first time, in this place, God Himself worked. They had read the normal mass, the bishop preached, and they had given us about thirty minutes to preach and pray for people. This was the time they planned to excommunicate us but they wanted to do it in front of the whole diocese. They said, "Preach like you do and pray." So I told another man, "Read the scripture – John 3:16 – and I will come and repeat the same thing. We will not do anything stupid here. If we do anything, our school is gone and we don't want people to fall. Just make everything short." They wanted us to do it as we do it in the Christian Union meetings. The bishop said, "I am now inviting our brother Jairus to come." The people in the back were shouting. The people in front were really watching us – so I never put my hands in my pockets. Father Queen had been coaching us, "Make sure your hands are straight out so they don't think you are doing some magic." He was at the far corner giving us a thumbs-up sign. "God will show that you are not doing your own things." I stood up slowly like a priest (with my robes on). "All of us here have heard the word of God. God loves us so much he doesn't want anyone to perish – that's why Christ came. Do you now believe in Him? If yes, you now have eternal life. I want us to pray now. Thank you, Lord, that you are going to show Yourself on our behalf." I handed the microphone to the bishop. He started to pray in the name of the Father, Son and Holy Spirit. People in the front started to fall. The more he said, "Ok," the more people were getting filled with the Holy Spirit. Father Queen said, "This is what I asked God to do. When you started, the bishop started." He tried to calm the people. Father Queen asked, "What is this? Maybe God is teaching something." "No, no, no. Not God. Bishop you are the one who prayed. Maybe they threw something to you. You should not have used that microphone." He called one of the elders to the front. He was Okemwa. "Even you – you are the one who was leading the group. What happened? What happened to you?" "Jesus came to me. Jesus talked to me about witchcraft and adultery." "You go." Another one. He found out these people were actually giving testimonies. Still others were crying out, making noise and crawling. Father Queen said, "Give the microphone to Jairus if you want quiet. I think he has that gift." He gave it to another priest from another parish, Father Lawrence Oseko. "Ok, come, come." The noise started again. "Jairus, do you know what is happening to the people?" They gave me the microphone. "Speak to them." Most of them who were making noise were youth. I said, "Praise the Lord! Hallelujah!" And they stopped.

They did not excommunicate us at that time because they did not have grounds. Before this, we used to go to many churches. Now we couldn't visit any other churches. Only the priests were allowed. I was banned from speaking to anyone at the college, except in class. One day we had a teacher – a professor from Catholic University, Nairobi— who came to lecture. When he came to class I did not know he had been told about me. "You young boys, you pretend to be holy, but you don't know anything. Jairus, today all your stupid questions will be answered. Ask one question or two that you think that are tough and you are going to get an answer now. Jairus, do you have a question?" "I'll ask after class," I replied. But he insisted, so I said, "I have a problem with one thing." "Yes, you have a problem!" "This is the problem and I thank you, Professor, for coming You are going to help me today and the whole class. I have the Bible and the catechism. This is my problem – the catechism and our Catholic Church teachings tell us that those people who died – Mary and others pray—for us. But in this Bible in the books of Romans and Hebrews it says that Christ is seated at the right hand and he makes intercession for us. Which of these two books is the truth and God's word? If I find the catechism is God's word, I only need the catechism. If the Bible is God's word, there are things in the catechism that I will not do."

"What is your name again? You say you have a problem with these two? This is a very small problem. Bishop, tell them which one is God's book. You know he has said he wants to leave one. He is right, when you are looking for truth you have to leave one." The

Bishop said, "End the class now. When you return after 30 minutes, we will give you the answer." But, the professor did not give an answer. Now the students demanded an answer. We were looking for an opportunity to burn the catechism. If they would say the Bible is the truth, we would burn the catechisms. The students were saying, "Ok, which one? This one or this one?" The Bishop said, "Jairus, you see what you have done in class?" I thought I'd finished during the first session. The Professor said, "Bishop, with your permission, let me answer this. The Bible is the word of God written for us. The catechism is the word of God through the church – so it's as good as the Bible, although the Bible is superior." The students said, "I'll take the superior one." The students dropped the catechisms and lifted the Bible higher. "Superior! Superior!" I knew everything would come against me. The Bishop called my parish priest and they said, "Pack up your things, Jairus. You go back home. You will come back to college when your priest tells us you have reformed."

Every time, my reformation was to denounce salvation, to say that I believed in a lie, there is no salvation, no Holy Spirit, I'd never been saved. They said, "You must do it through the priest first." Then they said I would need to go to the diocese and do the same. "You know, you are a priest – this is a small thing – just say the words from your mouth". Father Queen would come and say, "I've seen you out of the Catholic Church now – you can't make it here. I wish you could have stayed, but you are not going to make it. But don't run away – wait for the right time. Never, never deny Jesus, because you have received him!" We were a group of a hundred youth preaching everywhere.

Now that we were excommunicated from the church, about a hundred of us in Kisii district (which has now become 5 districts) would come and sit together. "Where do we go? What church do we go to? Let's form our own church. No, we don't know how to form one. We should go to an organized church and learn and then come back together again." But, then we scattered because we disagreed which group to join. (Our whole group have now become pastors and preachers). Each joined whichever church he saw fit. I myself and our congregation remained in the Catholic Church without a priest. We stayed in one place on a hill where we could pray on Sunday.

People came on Sunday, asking, "How now can we be baptized?" We only knew the Catholic way. When the priest heard we had a congregation, he went to the government District Office complaining we had split the church and were preaching wrong doctrines. They said that men, women and children sleep together the whole night (at *keshas*), that we needed to be arrested. They said our leader was Jairus. I was working with my two brothers. I did not like leadership positions. They accused, "One of them, Jairus, doesn't go to work in the shambas. He is encouraging people to uproot coffee, tea." (If you cut one you could be arrested.)

One day I was in the shamba – I had planted coffee, bananas, trees; I was busy working in that shamba. "Where is Jairus?" they demanded. I knew now I was in trouble. If people saw a policeman, everyone would disappear. "They are coming to shoot me," I thought. The whole village was saying, "Jairus, Jairus." "Where is Jairus who does not go to the farm?" "I'm the one," I said. "No. Where's your shamba?" I showed them the trees, coffee, bananas, sukuma wiki. "Do you have a problem with the church?" they asked. I told them how things were changing. "We have come to arrest you – let's go to the D.O.(District Officer)" The D.O. said, "These are the ones? Let's go see their shamba." We five young men were preaching together and also working together on our farms. They asked about men sleeping with women together. "No – it's an overnight prayer– called a *kesha*." In our area there wasn't a Pentecostal Church. We knew of only Aregio Marie that had things like *keshas*. The D.O. said, "You are doing everything right. Just don't use the Catholic name."

We were told we were an illegal group, so we sneaked away from home and went to Kitale to preach. The pastor who had invited us was from the Assemblies of God, but he was not saved. He said, "In our church we pay pastors and I don't have good school qualifications, so my father talked with my cousin who took me to Bible School so I could get some money." We said, "It's ok – the way you are preaching." He took us house to house preaching. We went to one house where there was a wizard woman who fell to the ground by the power of God. He was afraid that the woman was dead. But he said, "You are going to get arrested here if people start dying." No problem. We thought he understood what we were doing--that the power of evil was broken. The pastor left us, took his key, locked the house and left. We preached in the whole village. When we went back to the house, he was gone, and had left word for us to go away. He said it was dangerous. "People may die here. Some people may not resurrect. And I'll be responsible."

Now we didn't have a host. We went outside the church on the roadside. People came. I used to have a box guitar and funnel horns which we used as speakers so the sound would go far. When the people came, one of them got saved. He told us what the pastor had said. One woman from the Apostolic Faith church, whose husband had just died a few months before invited us to her house. Then the whole Apostolic Faith church came. We liked the name of this group. It was what we needed. We came back, announcing we were the Apostolic Faith Church; now we had a name. We never had a document or agreement with them, but we had taken the name. We invited them to take us in, so they took us in and we were re-baptized by immersion. We had not seen a declaration of faith, their beliefs, or government. We only knew the bishop. Later, we had another bishop, Bishop Musa from Nakuru who came to see us. When he came to Kisii he found us preaching. We loved this church. "Jairus, please come to Molo and be part of our team, Apostolic Faith Evangelistic Team." We joined that team. We didn't know there was infighting—that Musa had been elected out because he had changed the laws of the church without the right voting system. He had a theological degree and the others had not even gone to Bible School. Later they realized that he had changed the constitution so women didn't have to wear head scarves anymore. The older people complained and wanted to remove him. He brought the constitution and they found that it had been changed. Moses was general secretary of the Apostolic Faith group. At home we realized this church had a problem. They were very strict. You could not go to another region without the regional overseer going.

We wanted to have a church constitution. That's when we started telling Musa to bring a document so we could read and see it. Instead he brought the Church of God (New Testament Church of God) minutes. He had gotten it in Cleveland, Tennessee. So we went looking for Fred Brannen of the New Testament Church of God.

Musa already knew the Church of God when he was in America. When we looked at this book, we made copies for everyone. Everyone said this is the church we want. At that point, we joined the New Testament Church of God. From that time forth, I saw peace in the church. No one was interfering with the runnig of the church. That church would transfer me from place to place, from Molo to Kabatini, back to Molo, from Molo to Nakuru, back to Molo, from Molo to Elburgon, and then they wanted to transfer me to Nakuru again. Finally, I refused to go and I resigned.

By the time I came to Eldoret, I was a Church of God minister, pastoring an Apostolic Faith church! I was tricked to take care of the church for two weeks while the pastor went to London. From that day to this, he has never come back. I pastored that church with the help of another man who had come from London. He is now the senior pastor.

Life in the ministry has been tough, at times, but good. One of the churches I pastured in Nakuru had rich people. When I went there, I was by myself with my wife but the church's older men did not want a young man for a pastor. They wanted me out, but they did not want to use force. They wanted to starve me, so that we would leave. I remember for three or four days there was nothing in our house to eat. My wife and I decided to fast, although we did not have food, we decided to declare it a fast. One of the elders would come and see whether we had left, but he still found us there. We were going to fast for God to bring us food and money or a transfer out of that place. On the third day, we had only hot water on our table. We believed that if God could turn water into wine, he could also change this water into food in our bodies. When we put the water there, we were giving thanks for the water. To our amazement, there came a knock at the door. When we opened the door, there were men and women from Molo who had come to visit us. They brought us food enough for a whole month: charcoal, milk and sugar. "We just came; show us the kitchen!" They took over the kitchen and we ate together. We said, "We have seen God." From that time, the elders changed. They came and saw we had everything. We asked them to call the other elders. All of us ate and there was more than enough. One of the elders said, "This man cannot go. If we don't give them food, it will come from another place." They started blessing us, supporting us fully.

When I went to Elburgon, the people were very poor. Every time it came to giving they would say, "Oh, we are poor." But whenever I visited them, they had something to put on the table, and actually the food was good and expensive. So, I decided to help them see that they were rich. The problem was "giving" in the church—not at home. So I decided to talk about it in the church, but in a nice way. I said, "What happens? When we are at home, we have money. When a visitor comes to our house, we can feed them. What happens when we come to church, when we are to give for the ministry? How do we get rich at home? We say we are so poor and cannot give anything in the church. We are going to give a small amount in the church because we are poor and cannot manage to buy even a small piece of land or pay rent. And it seems that only I, the pastor, give for the rent." Someone in the congregation who was relatively poor was one I had visited. She actually bought good food, so I was using her as an example. I told them she bought me food and all these things and it was worth much money. She stood and testified and said that every time she came to church, she thought it was not a good place to give. No one said, "thank you," when someone gave. In the church, the presence of people seeing you do the right thing was not there. At home, if you don't give food, they laugh at you. In the church no one applauds and says you have done well. She confessed that she realized that she was not poor. She didn't realize the pastor was watching her to see what she was giving compared to others. I agreed. When I stood at the offering basket, people gave more money. I realized when I was not there to watch, they gave very little. So, I asked, "Do you see the difference? When I am not standing there you give less. Am I in the place of God? We need to realize that He is watching what we give." From then on, they started giving their money. When we wanted to buy land, I said, "Only the rich will give," and no one wanted to remain in the poverty class.

One of the most challenging times in ministry has involved the clashes. In 1992 there were clashes in Rift Valley, including Molo. The victims came running to the City Social Hall, which we were renting for services. We did not have a place to hold our services, and every time we went there we saw how the children and elderly were suffering.

We were unable to provide for them as a church except to help a few people with food stuffs. We could not help the majority. I remember that we would go there and cry with them, instead of helping, because we didn't have anything to give. On Sunday, we wanted to move them out so we could have church, but they had some of their property, which they had carried with them. They didn't want to leave without their possessions, and they were weak and hungry. It was a challenging time to have to tell people to go out because we wanted to have a service. After they took out all of their property, they came back in. Most were the same people we said we needed to help. Then they said, "The church is saying they will help us, so we are not moving from the church." They thought we were just staying there. They said, "We'll just wait here (at the altar) for help." We decided to go home and look for food so we could help this one family that we thought was the most affected. We came back and handed the food to that man. But, we soon realized that everyone wanted the food, so the people grabbed the food from that man, and by the time we left there, he was almost hurt, because people were pulling and trying to get the food. We realized we were not helping, because it was so little. So we went to ask the government and Red Cross to get help.

But the worst violence was in 2007 in Eldoret. People ran to our church just when we were about to run away also. The church started to raise money, but it wasn't enough. They began to leave when they had no more money to give. We did not have food because even the little we had we had shared with the people. We thought it was a day's problem, but it persisted for a whole year. This is the time when we had about 1500 people in our church compound without food. I remember one old man who was once rich, but who during the clashes lost everything. He sat under a tree and he did not want to talk to anybody. I thought he was resting and did not have any problem, because he was nicely dressed. He did not want to eat anything, but while we were serving the people, he collapsed. When he collapsed, somebody said, "It is because he lost everything. He was very rich and he lost everything and I think he is dead." We took him to my house and prayed for him and we started singing songs of hope because I didn't have a way to get him to hospital, because no one wanted to go on the roads. There were no vehicles and everyone was afraid to move on the roads. Later, he sat down and said, "Have they destroyed my house? That is my whole life's savings." He had worked all his life to enjoy that house. Now he felt like he had lost everything, but I asked him," If you had died and the house remained, which is better, my house, or a mud house? Is your being alive worth more than a house?" He said, "Yes." "And is not life more precious than any wealth you could acquire?" He stood up and ate. After awhile he went to another camp in Nakuru.

One of the challenges that we faced was that babies were born at the church without nurses. My wife was the one acting as hostess and making sure the children were safe and warm, and by the grace of God none of the children died. We had about 18 children born at the church. By the grace of God and with the help of the brethren, we were able to provide them clothes and bedding.

One problem at the very beginning concerned latrines. We had only one that was subdivided into two rooms – one for women and one for men, but when the people came, within two days it was full and they didn't have anywhere to go. We didn't have people to dig or materials for them to use to build another. Finally, we started digging another latrine, thinking the clashes would end in a short time. It was about 10 feet deep and we thought it would last us two or three weeks at least, but it was already full in two days. The whole area was full of flies. It was a mess. I prayed that people would not contract cholera. We were praying, and at the same time, we realized we needed to be digging all the time. Some of the Internally Displaced People tried to help us dig. But, whenever they dug, they asked me for money. I didn't have anything to pay them. They needed food. Eventually, the Red Cross and others helped us dig latrines which they covered with polyethylene sheets. Though these latrines were not very clean, they helped the situation until we were able to dig bigger and deeper latrines. Because there were so many people in the place and many children, often they could not wait their turn for a latrine and ended up using open ground as a latrine. The church compound became very bad-smelling. Flies became pests and it was a great challenge to spray the whole compound against them. But, God helped us so that none of our children or our church camp was sick. No one died.

Another problem was discipline of the camp. I did not want

people to fight between different tribes and ethnic groups. Each group was suspicious of the others. I didn't want people to be identified by their names because their names showed which tribe someone came from. I had the people give only their first name with a number – without their second name. We had people from one community come two times to ask if their enemies were in the camp. I would say, "No." I would bring people from their own community and show them their people were there and they would go and get food to feed them. I used that to bring about unity among the people. Actually people were quite disciplined. I told them we were Lighthouse Camp and that we would speak only the national language, Kiswahili. That discipline helped us.

But there were other problems. One couple gave birth to twins in the camp. When the woman gave birth to these two children, because they were poor and did not have food, they decided to sell one of the twins, so they could buy food and help the other child to live. Then we heard that one lady friend of ours had given birth, so we went to visit. My wife recognized the baby; that baby was one of the twins. We went to see the parents of the twins to check whether they had the two children, and we found out they had only one. We involved their parents plus the police to get the child back from the one who had bought the other twin. The child was then returned to the parents and the Red Cross took over from there to help that family to bring up the children in a different way.

As a result of the clashes, we now have two more children who are part of our family. My children learned to appreciate other children and to be grateful for what they have. The violence affected my mother also, who was living with us. Every time she heard a loud noise, she became disturbed. My oldest daughter was unable to go to school because the roads were blockaded and I had to change her to another school. This has affected her academic performance. Another one of the results was that financially we were affected, because we used all the money we had personally, and the church's money as well. We still have not fully recovered. Some of the refugees stayed on as part of the church. Some of our members who left the church have come back recently, but some have never returned.

My vision for the future is "peace-building" in our community, so that we don't have the same occurrence in the future. We go to communities once every two months holding inter-tribal meetings, where we ask people to share why they need to learn to live together as one. This started as a small group, but now we have non-governmental and governmental groups that help us. I'm the religious representative in our area.

LOST BOY
Gabriel Chol Pareng

Many years ago when the sun disappeared for awhile and stars suddenly appeared, my grandfather Chol was born. Years later I was given the same name, meaning "compensation" because he made up for the loss of an earlier child. However, I wasn't compensating for anyone. When I arrived in 1973, I was the first born. Our home was in Bor (one of eleven counties in the state of Jongle), Southern Sudan, in a little village called Kolnyang. Now it is developing as the headquarters of the county of Payam, but at that time it was insignificant.

Before my mother could have another child, she died from a disease similar to chronic malaria – probably hepatitis. Our people say that her eyes and fingernails turned green. Since I was only two years old, my need for care was met by my grandma, with whom I went to live. At first my father refused to marry again. But, because he was also a first-born, the younger brothers forced him to marry so that he would have to take responsibility for the old parents. My grandfather and grandmother were still alive. Now my father had two wives, and if you include my mom, he has had three. The youngest wife spent about six years without having a child, until I brought them to Kenya. She now has a daughter and the middle wife has six daughters, followed by a boy of 12 years old, born in 1998. Now he is with me, also, and since he is the only brother, I have to take care of him.

My life in Sudan was greatly affected by war. The first major war in Sudan, "Anyanya I" started in 1951. This war began shortly after the independence of Sudan. When things didn't work right after independence, the southerners decided to claim their separate independence. I was born in the midst of that war, which ended when a Disababa Accord was signed in 1979. During that war people used to run and hide in the bushes because the Arabs were attacking villages, raiding cows and plundering the commodities like grain, etc. The Arabs were trying to change people's minds, to convert them to Islam. Because people refused conversion, the Arabs were mistreating people.

We lived in a mud house with a grass roof. My father was a cattle keeper and also a farmer. He raised sim sim (a seed similar to sunflower seeds) and small white beans. They were planted together, but harvested by hand at different times. A sickle was used to cut the sim sim very carefully without damaging the grain. Afterwards the sickle was again used to cut off the seeds. After the sim sim was dried, it was threshed and then it was fried dry because it contains oil like peanuts. Afterwards it was ground. Sometimes it was mixed with beans. They would add only salt or salt and water to make a soup.

I was raised to be a cattle keeper. My father, grandfather, and great grandfather before him were all chiefs of our village. People lived together and I was not raised any differently from any of the other children. However, if I mistreated someone, or I acted badly, I would be reminded that I was the son of the chief. If I was given something to eat, I could not eat alone. I was told that I must share with others.

I went to school in 1979 because the last born of my grandfather was educated and insisted that I should be educated also. He enrolled me to school in Kolyang, but my father was refusing for me to go to school because I was to be his cattle keeper. My uncle won out and I went to school. We started our school under a tree. I completed the whole of class one under that tree. By the time I went to my second year, we had a mud house with a grass roof for classes 2, 3 and 4. While I was in class four, in 1983, the second war broke out. We ran and hid when the villages were attacked. The war escalated until in 1987 our cattle were attacked and people ran in different directions.

I found myself without my parents. I teamed up with a group of thousands of people and we began walking to Ethiopia. I didn't know where we were going, but some of the leaders knew. At 14 years of age I became a refugee. We have been called the "Lost Boys" because we were without our parents. If I can remember correctly, we traveled for 2 ½ to 3 months. We slept in the bushes. When our leaders felt we should sleep, we stopped. If we were in the village of a certain tribe, we would take our clothes and exchange them for food. If my clothes were used to exchange one day, another's would be used the next day. Sometimes we ate leaves and seeds from the trees when there were no people to trade with. When we reached Ethiopia we were naked. We stayed there for half a month until UNHCR came and we had clothes to wear again. These long walks were very hard on us. On the way, my feet swelled and sometimes I didn't know if I'd be able to walk in the morning. But there seemed to be nothing to do but to walk. Sometimes we were afraid of wild animals like lions and hyenas. When the older ones decided we should sleep, we lit fires to keep us warm, and the older ones took turns keeping watch. We rubbed sticks together to start the fires. If we got sick on the way, there was no medicine, so many people died on the way. However, none of my closest friends died. If it was a large forest, where we could not exchange clothes or find food, hunger became a real problem. We also feared certain people, particularly, a tribe called Murle who were ones who abducted children. When we passed through their villages we were afraid that we would be abducted. They still do this. I don't know why. In 2009, they took the child of my sister-in-law and adopted him by force.

After reaching Ethiopia, we had about a month without food and shelter until the UNHCR came and visited us. When they visited us, we became afraid because they were red and white people, so we thought they were Arabs. We ran when we saw them. After one week many trucks came full of food and clothes. They gave us big quilts to keep us warm at night. We started building our shelters. We were given tools, like axes to cut the grass and the trees to make the shelters. The Ethiopians were very short and red (especially Eritreans) and we feared them, also, thinking they were cannibals. We lived in terror of these people and animals. When the Eritreans would go around with salt to sell, we thought they were exploring our place and they would come at night to kill us. I don't know what brought those thoughts into our minds. We stayed there from 1987 to 1991.

At the end of that time, war broke out in Ethiopia. Mgisto was overthrown and those who overthrew him were trained in Sudan by the Khartoum government. When we reached Pibor in the midst of the Murle, we were given SPLA soldiers to escort us. But we became afraid of the Khartoum government and ran back to Sudan. When we came to the border there was a river called the Ghilo River. During that crossing, many people who didn't know how to swim were drowned. The Ethiopian military people ran after us and the Khartoum government started bombing us as we entered Southern Sudan. Because of that bombing from the air, we had to hide by day and take our journey by night. That is how my right eye was "bitten" by a thorn one night as we were walking through the forest alongside the river. As we were walking by night, the lions were roaring. When we ran from them, we went through the thorn bushes. I couldn't tell anyone or cry aloud because maybe the lions would hear me. I quietly told a friend that I had had an accident. Immediately I saw many colors before my eyes and it was very painful. My friends took me by the hand and led me to a settlement. Now I was really in trouble, because I had gotten measles when I was six months old and it had affected my left eye. My father said I hadn't been able to see for about three months. Now both eyes were hurt.

After having this accident on the way, I was taken care of by my friends who were with me until we came to a place called Kapoita, one of the main centres of Eastern Equatorial State. After a month that town was captured by the Khartoum government. The time was 1992. We had to run again, this time toward the Kenyan border. We settled in Lokochokio for two months and finally ended up in Kakuma.

Life in the Kakuma Refugee Camp was hard because it is a desert – very humid and very hot with too much wind. Even by day the vehicles needed to use lights because of the dust. Again we had to build houses. We were given poles, plastic sheets and *makuta* (palm-type branches) to cover the plastic sheets for a roof. The walls and floor were made of mud. The camp officials dug wells and used pumps to bring water to the camp which contained thousands of refugees. There were refugees from Ethiopia, Uganda, Somalia, Ruanda, the Congo, as well as Sudan. It has become the main refugee camp in East Africa. UNHCR distributed food items twice a month on the 1st and 15th of each month. We were given cards and each individual received a bi-monthly ration. If you were the head of a family, you were given food for the whole family. We, who were without families, put our food together and shared the food, fuel and worked together.

When we ran from our village to Ethiopia, I felt there was no hope that I would be back in Sudan again, or that I would ever find my parents. When I had the accident with my eye, I didn't think I could get an education or do anything for myself. However, I always had a desire to learn the Word of God. When I enrolled in 1979 in the school there was teaching of Christian Religious Education. That teacher was a good Bible teacher, so I came to hear about God. We had a chapel in the school where they used to teach songs and Bible verses. After I ran to Ethiopia there was a pastor named Andrew Mayol, who also came about a year later than us to the refugee camp. He helped us a lot. Many people were sick mentally to the extent that many people went insane. But he counseled us and that was when I was baptized. I decided to believe Christ as my personal Savior. I was taught by that pastor and baptized by him in 1989.

That pastor is the one who imparted a lot of things to me. After I had my accident, he also ran with us to Sudan, and stayed with us as a pastor. He even ran with us to Kenya.

In primary school, CRE (Christian Religious Education) was a lesson, but even as a child I loved the church. I was the song leader and looked forward to worship. When war broke out I lost hope until that pastor came to Ethiopia and raised my faith again.

When I had the accident to my eye, I didn't know if I could be effective again in the church or even be able to make a life for myself. However, in Kakuma, the pastors and others brought me in and I became involved in the ministry. I became youth leader in 1998 and then I was selected by the church to attend Malek Bible School in Kakuma. I studied for nine months in that Bible School. When I had studied for those nine months, with only three months remaining of my Bible School, our bishop in Nairobi decided to let the teachers move from one displaced camp to another. After Kakuma, I went back to Sudan to the displaced person's camp in a place called Nimuli. I finished the last three months of Bible School there. I tried to find my parents but was unable. However, I heard about them – that my Dad was alive and all my step brothers and sisters and step mother were alive except for one sibling (sister) who had died after I left. But I didn't meet them.

In 1999 I went back to Bor and was reunited with my father and siblings. Going to Bor from Nimuli was hard – we had to go to Juba and then circle around, crossing the Nile River from west to east. It took me two months. (Now we could do it in 1 ½ days from Eldoret). What a joyous reunion we had! My father was not even aware that I was alive. I just surprised him. I arrived in the village on Saturday evening, around six, but I couldn't get to his house, so I slept in the church. In the morning I conducted the service. I was hoping he would come to the church. After the church, I had to go to where my family was staying, but I couldn't find him until I went to the nearby houses in the village. They showed me where my father had built his family home. I found out that all the people in the church and my family had gathered to meet me. People were celebrating, singing and dancing. They killed a big ram for us to eat. It was prepared for me alone, but I said, "Let everyone sit and we will eat together." We prayed and thanked God for the reunion. I spent about a year there teaching and preaching in the church. That was a joyous time for me to be in our homeland. They licensed me to be a lay leader in the Anglican Church – to preach and teach and assist the priest in the service. It had been 12 years since I had left my father.

At that point, I returned to Kakuma. I realized that the church had seen something in me, so I decided to come and pursue my education to know the Word better. I wanted to do some more courses. When I had my accident, I didn't know if I could do something – but now I saw that they believed I could be of service. Because they were giving me many responsibilities, I needed to learn more.

My father suggested I take a wife then, but I was not ready for that. When I came back to Kakuma, I got sick and my uncle – the last born of my grandmom, who had left our village to go to Khartoum and eventually had become educated in England-- somehow heard that a relative of his (myself) was in Kakuma. The brother-in-law of this uncle had relatives in Kakuma with me. Through these relatives he heard about my sickness and since he was a doctor he was concerned and said that I should come to see him in Eldoret, Kenya. He was working with Sudan.

Medical Care, an NGO in Southern Sudan, but his family was in

Eldoret. So I came to Eldoret to meet him and stay with him.

During my treatment, I joined with people who were in Eldoret and we started a fellowship. We worshipped from house to house until a house was not big enough to hold all of us, so we called one of our pastors in Nairobi and he talked to the Catholics who gave us a facility to use from 2002 until 2005. That year a new Catholic priest came and he chased us away. The pastor that was transferred was Irish and because of problems in Ireland, it seems he didn't like us (Anglicans) being there.

I was just looking around Kapsoya to see if I could find a church. I didn't notice Lighthouse Church because it was not finished. After failing to find a venue, I came to Pastor Jairus Mosoti, who received us to worship in that church. Many churches had said we could come, but when it came time to meet, they weren't there. One day I was praying that if I couldn't get a church that day I would go to St. Matthew's, but that church was very far. After that I put my collar on and went to Jairus' church. The only person I found in the church was his little daughter. When she saw me, she ran away. I followed her and clapped my hands and Jairus came out. When I came, I asked him if it was the pastor's house. "Yes," he replied. "Is he in?" "Yes." I told him the issue, that I was looking for a place for our people to use as a place of worship. He said, "You are welcome." "Are you the pastor?" "Yes."

We went to the church building together to see it. We exchanged information. I told him that I was an Anglican pastor. He said, "People won't go to heaven by denomination or organizations but by faith." That was his reply, which really fascinated me. I was amazed at the way he received me. From then on, I appreciated him. I like to say he is "kingdom-minded" because his faith is beyond denominational boundaries. (You can read Jairus' story elsewhere in this book.)

Through Pastor Jairus I came to be at Discipleship College, a college that has impacted my life. In all this, I thank God for what he has done.

Before I came to Discipleship College, I attended another school run by Mark Franz for three months. Then I decided to go back to Sudan to visit my family again. My uncle who was in England talked to his sister in Australia to send me there. But I was rejected, and another person was sent. I decided to go and tell my parents goodbye in 2006. Coming back, I came to find out that the Australian government had sent me a rejection letter because of my eye problem. So I had to go back to Sudan again, at which point my father said, "Since you are not going anywhere, you will be given a wife." So, I said, "Let me go back to where I was before." But he objected, thinking I might refuse again. I wrote to my friends in the church to look for me a wife. This is how I found my wife, Tabitha Ayen. One of my friends recommended her and I went with the company of my relatives to see if this would be the one. They also agreed, so we decided to marry.

After I married her, we had a pastor's conference for two weeks in 2007 and I was appointed by the senior pastor to attend that workshop. During that time, I managed to get a friend from the USA, one of the teachers who taught in the workshop. That friend arranged for my visit to the USA because of my eye problem. After the conference in America, he took me to three hospitals, but the result was that it was too late for them to do anything about my eye. One was John Hopkins University Hospital. They said the nerves were gone. After realizing that there was no hope again for me to see better, God encouraged me by giving me a decision that if this little vision could still remain, I could study more to help the church by spreading the Gospel.* I shared that with some of my friends in the US, and that's how I ended up with someone who is assisting me until now with my education. When I came from the US, I was looking for a place to study. It was then that Jairus encouraged me to come to Discipleship College and I thank God for that.

After enrolling in this school, I decided to go and get my wife to bring her here, because it is hard to be alone and it would be difficult for me to go and come from Sudan for four years. A better way was to bring her closer to me so that she could assist me in many ways and so that I could be responsible for her. We now have two precious daughters, Mary (5) and Deborah (2).

My desire is to return to Sudan to establish a church there where I can train young people to spread the Gospel. My heart is to teach people about the Word of God.

* To read Gabriel must put the book within two inches from his eyes. He only needs to read things once. He has trained himself to remember what he reads. He uses every bit of the sight that remains.

SNATCHED FROM A CULT
Nicas Wasike Nyakuri

Unlike most Kenyan boys, I was circumcised at the tender age of 8 days. You see, I was born into a cult called the Lost Israel of Kenya. This cult, which had attracted 5,000 adherents, was led by a man called Jehovah Wanyonyi, whom we considered "God." Our family of ten made its home in Kimalewa, Western Province. All of us followers lived in a camp which was secluded from other people. I grew up believing that we were the real Israel who were displaced from the country of Israel and exiled in Kenya. We dressed like the old traditional Jews and practiced traditions of the Jewish religion. Our strict beliefs separated us from the world and people whom we called the "people of the nations," and whom we considered extremely worldly. The followers of our cult sold everything we had, shared with the poor among us and some of the possessions we gave to our leader. Amassing of possessions was not

Tea Without Sugar: Chastened for a Destiny

allowed because we believed that soon we would leave the world. We didn't build permanent shelters for the same reason.

When I was few weeks old my dad became sick and was forced to move from this camp to Mount Elgon where he was treated by my maternal parents. Life in the camp did not favor people who were sick. Members survived by working for a daily wage to have food on the table. My grandparents had acquired the property in Mount Elgon for free because it was a forest. When my parents came in they just cleared the forest 5 miles away from my Grandparent's home to have land. We lived in Mount Elgon for some years, but my parents were still strong believers in this cult. When I was only one year old I went to stay with my maternal grandparents because my brother had come so quickly. My parents had to give me to my grandmom to take care of me while they were taking care of my little brother. *In my grandparent's home* I was introduced to the Catholic denomination where I regularly attended Sunday services.

I remember there was a Catholic priest called Father John. He was a Catholic missionary from Italy. He strongly impacted my life and I loved him so much for what he was doing with the kids. I was really inspired by the Bible stories he told us. I remember one day when I was still 3 years old, I visited my parents to stay with them for a few days. During my stay there, one night outside our house in the moonlight I knelt down and I started praying. I was unaware that people were watching me from the house. I made my best prayer that night asking God to show his grace to us. When I finished my dad came to me. He angrily told me that we don't pray to the God who is in heaven. He then said that they worship a god they see. He told me about Jehovah Wanyonyi. But from that time, I knew there was something wrong with my parents' beliefs. I hesitated but did not oppose them because I knew I would get some beatings for doing that.

Despite very many hardships in my grandmother's home she did everything to provide for me. I went to nursery school when I was 3 years old. My teacher was called John Wafula. He was such a good teacher; he taught me to read and write. From the start, my best book was the Bible, not any other book in the house. He encouraged me to work hard in everything I did and I did not disappoint him. I was the best in my class.

One day I was very sick and my grandma thought I was going to die. She took me to the hospital which was two days walking distance from the forest where we stayed. (We lived in the place called Jepteka and the nearest hospital was in a place called Kapsakwany - 30 miles away). The place was hard to pass through because of its mountainous nature. The means of transport there was donkeys. (I first saw a car when I was the age of 8 years. I was 10 when I first rode in one). Something dramatic happened while we were still on the way to the hospital. A drunkard man emerged from the forest and got hold of my grandmom's hand. She was afraid but he said, "I don't want to harm you. I just came to tell you that this boy you are carrying on your back is not going to die because he will be a servant of God." Since that time my grandmom was watching me to see if that would be fulfilled. I remember 14 years later she gave her life to Jesus. When she realized that I was a saved Christian, she abandoned smoking tobacco. That day I was coming from school and I felt so bad for my grandmom, so I was praying for her. I knew how hard it would be for her to leave tobacco. She had tried many times, but had always come back to smoking. I really thought it was demonic because she began in response to a dream in which she was told that she should smoke. When we tried to talk to her about being born again and giving up her cigarettes, which we would burn, my granddad would tell me, "You will be the one to buy her tobacco when you see her start dying." But this time, she was able to leave the tobacco completely. My granddad still confesses up to now that my grandma's leaving smoking was dramatic to him, though he has not joined her in her new church. From then on, my grandma was delivered from smoking and she became a prayerful and committed Pentecostal Christian.

My parents' stay with my grandparents was short-lived. My parents moved back to Kimalewa to be in the camp with other cult followers. Meanwhile I was left in my grandparents' home.

Again the government of Kenya chased all people that were living in the forest to look for another home since the forest was taken over by the government. It was a setback to my parents for they were left without any home. We moved to Bungoma. We stayed like refugees for some time with no home. The change of location affected me very much. I became very sickly from malaria. By contrast, in

Mount Elgon there were not many cases of malaria because it is cold. Because of my frequent bouts with malaria, my mom came and took me back to Kimalewa to stay with them in the camp.

When I was 9 years old I already realized the benefit of being in school so I did anything I could to go to school. Life was not so easy for me. I got a lot of opposition from my dad from the start. In the cult the children, too, were forced to go to work on the farms. As a group, we used to wake up at 4 am in the morning, walk for miles looking for someone who would give us work to do on a farm for that day. In return we were usually given 2 kilograms of maize for a day's work and the rest was given to their god. Sometimes we did not have a job and so we had no food at all since our work was seasonal and the cult did not store food. I remember one time we went without food for two weeks. We survived on a weed called jack. It is a little bitter but it kept us alive.

I really had a desire to have education. But to avoid the conflicts with my parents, I would go to work for some days and when I got the opportunity I would go to school secretly. When there were fewer jobs then I would seize the opportunity and go to school twice a week and work on the farms sometime four days a week. The seventh day was a Sabbath when everybody went to worship. Thank God I had very good teachers who understood my situation except one who gave me a lot of headaches. He would make me kneel down and walk on my knees imitating what we usually did when we were worshipping this man. But wonder of all wonders, even though I missed school so often, I used to be the best student in my class. I remember from Standard Two to Eight, I used to be Position One.

It became clear that I was rebelling against what my parents wanted and the situation got worse, so that my going to school was marred with a lot of hardship. Lunch for me was just a vocabulary word. To avoid being a laughing stock in front of my fellow school mates, I would pretend that I was going for lunch, but I just went somewhere to drink water and came back to school for evening classes. Many kids could not understand why I missed lunch. I became so bitter about everything that I even wanted to commit suicide. But God did not allow me do it. One day in the year 1994 I was preparing for my primary final exam. Things were hard for me because there was no food at all. We were back to black jack for food again in order to survive. That day I thank God my dad was not at home. Men in the camp that period went to work at a construction site in some far place for half a year. I came home that evening and was very angry at my mother. I asked her many questions. Why were we passing through this even though they were adherent worshippers? She did not have an answer. Instead, she cried, too.

The following day I did not go to school. I had lost hope in everything. I wanted to die. I remember making a prayer that night before that if God would not allow me or give me the strength to go to school I had better die. The following day I did not go to school; at first I wanted to be alone to commit suicide by drowning in the river called Kuywa. While on the way to the river God miraculously provided a company of young people who were going to fish and they convinced me to go fishing. They even provided me with a fishing hook and line. We tried to get fish for four hours with no success. Not one of us had successfully gotten even a single fish. But when we were just about giving up, I took my last chance. I threw my hook in one last time. Suddenly I felt on my hook a strong pull that pulled me into the water. It was a very big fish. My friend helped me to get it out and on our way home I met with one of my lady teachers who was coming from school. She asked me why I did not come to school. I explained and finally she bought the fish at 130 shillings. That amount of money at that time would buy almost a sack of maize for food. I saved my mother and my siblings with enough food to carry for three weeks.

In November, 1994, I did my final primary school exam. I was the best in school with a grade of A and the following year I was chosen to attend either Chesamis High School or Kamsinga High School. These are the best schools in western province. I was given only one week to report to the schools or my chance would be taken. Indeed, it was taken away because there was no one to pay my fees. That week before the dead line to these schools, I tried to go to places to get money. One of my elder sisters gave me two thousand shillings. But they needed seven thousand for school start fees, not counting all of the other supplies and personal things I would need. I could not make it so I just quit. I did not know what to do next. But, it seems to be human nature that if your own effort fails you, run to God or a higher being. That night I went to my knees again. I told God if only this time He would help me, then I would live to show his greatness. In the following morning my father realized that I had two thousand shilling and he wanted to take that money away. But I refused and threatened that I would rather die than let the money get away. I went to bed that night contemplating suicide, but in the following morning I had peace of mind that I had never had in my life. I was so happy, something in me was compelling me to go take a *matatu* (van used for public transportation) and go! I did not know where I was going. I told my parents and my siblings that I was going away and I remember my dad saying, "We have lost him." He said that I was not his son anymore.

I felt disowned but I was so happy while going away. I bought a *matatu* ticket to Kitale town. Arriving in Kitale I recalled my sister telling me that there were relatives in a place called Moi's Bridge. I did not know the place. The moment I arrived in Mois Bridge, I met my uncle. His name is Peter Kakai. He was coming from a mission in Mount Elgon. He had left Mt. Elgon when I was still young so for 8 years we had never met. He was happy to see me and because he understood where I came from he was willing to take me to Kiptoim secondary school in Baringo South. He took me in by faith because on his part, too, he had a lot of financial responsibilities.

Kiptoim secondary school was a very poor school with very few facilities. The school academically was also very poor. No one in school had ever made grades to qualify for university. I was determined that I would make it to break the record. Due to my hard working in class I got the highest share of bursary funds from the government. One good thing about the school was the level of Christianity which was very high at that particular time. For me it was like a Bible college and I became one of the Bible study coordinators in my group. The school helped me to build my Christian foundation. By the time I came out of school I was a praise and worship leader and a preacher.

One of my problems in secondary school was that I had no place during break because my uncle was single and a traveling preacher, I couldn't go to my parents, so usually I just stayed at school, where sometimes people would help me a little. My elder sister was the only person I would sometimes visit but she was not a Christian and her husband was a drunkard. Their situation troubled me so much that for some time I didn't visit them. I remember when I was in Form Two I went and visited her. But when I was there I became very sick, and my tongue started swelling. Many people from the Luhya community believe these kinds of diseases are due to witchcraft. They believe that after three days one will be dead. Because of my beliefs, I refused to go to the witch doctor and I even refused to take traditional medicine. My condition grew worse and I could see the fear of my sister who was crying. She believed that I would be dead after three days. But that very night when I was expected to be dead, God healed me and I woke up feeling alright and there was not any kind of swelling of my tongue. It was the first dramatic thing that Jesus did for me. Years later, my sister remembered my healing and surrendered her life to Jesus. Every time she goes to church she testifies about her little brother and how Jesus healed him and opened eyes when she was too blind to see. Her husband really had a battle leaving drinking. I asked how he would leave that life. Recently, he got very sick and the choice was to die or to leave drinking. He chose to live. This, too is a miracle.

Another miracle happened when I was with my grandma. At that time she was not Christian; I was very sick with malaria. But every day I would walk very early in the morning before the sun rose, and run to my church called Redeemed Gospel to pray. There was no money to buy drugs. When I got very sick one morning I started "kicking the bucket." I lost all my energy and I was unconscious for some time. During that time I made one prayer, I told God, "If it is your will for me to die, I am thankful because I am coming to you," and I told the devil that he was the loser forever. When I finished this prayer, God healed me. I regained energy, became conscious and woke up only to find many people crying because I was dead. I did not go to hospital because God had healed me completely. From that day my grandma gave her life to Jesus. She told me about what had happened sometime before, back in Mount Elgon, during the time when she was taking me to hospital.

I was a very lonely man is high school. One reason was that during visiting days no one came to see me. I became bitter about my parents. I started thinking that God didn't care at all. Though I was bitter about everything I did not give up on God. This bitterness toward my parents was over when I met a teacher called Andrew Russo, who helped me out of this. I learned that bitterness is not godly; it keeps one in bondage, and stops blessings from God. So I forgave my parents and from that time I have always tried to have a good relationship with them.

In 1999, I did my final exam in high school. I was the best student, the first one attaining a grade that could get one to university. Finishing high school was the biggest miracle for me. Because of my good foundation in Christianity, I prayed that I would get a church that would help me to serve. In the following year in Eldoret Pastor Daniel Chelagat told me he was planning to plant a church. He had just finished his studies in the US and came purposefully to plant a church in Eldoret. He, being a good friend of my uncle, asked my uncle to help him get young people that would help him in worship leadership. My uncle chose me and one lady from my school. We joined three other young people to do praise and worship in a new church called Pioneer Community Church. I was so happy to serve in full time ministry just like I had promised God. In Pioneer Community Church Pastor Daniel Chelagat was my mentor for five years. I led praise and worship and also I was youth leader.

I worked very hard in whatever I did; I was a praise and worship leader, playing any kind of instrument that was in my way. I played drums, the keyboard, guitar, and other instruments. Working in Pioneer Community Church was a blessing to me. I was exposed to and taught how to do evangelism, preach and many other things pertaining to ministry.

After two years in service, I felt that God was calling me for higher things and I needed some training. By faith, I went to Discipleship College which was a distance learning center of Lee University to do a Bachelor's Degree in Christian Ministry. My four year experience taught me to be a man of faith in God. I always make big steps by faith because I know if it is God's will it is bound to succeed.

In the year 2007 I finished my Christian Ministries education in college and God provided Patten University to do Music and Worship Leadership, which I am gladly doing with all my energy. I thank God for this. In this entire God has been teaching me how to love. He has taught me patience and endurance when things are tough. I can say like Joseph in the Bible that they meant it for other reasons but God meant is for good. I believe every Christian is obligated to be the best he can be for God. God will pass people through circumstances so that they are refined and are taught in such a way that their ministry is improved. God will always prepare His people for the higher service. One author has said "God's army most of the time are not trained in the king's palace, they are trained in the wilderness. They are always found tending sheep like David and Moses in the desert."

I have learned also that there are areas in life where we are supposed to walk alone. We don't need to lean on anyone or anything but God. Christians are called to be leaders who are always ahead of their followers. Being ahead in most cases leads to loneliness. Enoch in the Bible walked alone with God, Noah and his family in the midst of a perverse generation walked with God. Just like He did with Noah, in the loneliest times God speaks his plans and his secrets into our lives. In my life God has used these moments when I am lonely to speak his love, to confirm the ministry he has placed in my heart. Loneliness seems to me to be the price a man or woman of God needs to pay for his godliness. Hardship seems to be a good teacher that God uses to let us know and discover the depth of His love for us.

I believe that God has called all Christians to be the light of the world. This higher calling was not for our benefit only but for the benefit of others who are still in darkness. Our Lord's great commission was that we go into the world and make disciples. I love the words from J. Oswald Sanders in his book Spiritual Leadership:

> *If the world is to hear the church's voice today, leaders are needed who are authoritative, spiritual and sacrificial. Authoritative because people will hear others who are in control and know where they are going, spiritual because without God's power even the most attractive person or wise person cannot lead people to God. Sacrificial because it follows our Lord Jesus' model, he 'died' for his flock.*

Many young people fear to take any step in life to improve their standard of life because there seems to be no way. Looking at where God has brought me from, I feel like I can encourage some of them.

This is the kind of people my heart is crying for. For seven years I have been doing the ministry, reaching out to the young people in Africa. I started with my brothers and sister who are now all born again Christians. One of my brothers is now a pastor in a local church.

With the meager amount of money I get, I pay school fee for my two sisters. One is in high school and the other in primary school.

I still have problems with my parents concerning the education of my sister but now-a-days we have human rights and police can put my father in "check" if he raises the alarm over the issue. I have gone as far as trying to rescue the kids from this cult. I am in contact with some and I try to help and teach them the importance of going to school.

Six years ago, we formed a youth group called NARWA (Nasangali Reformed Welfare Association). We come together twice a year to learn much about life issues. We encourage each other to be God fearing, to work hard so as to improve our economic status. We come together to help those who are going to school. Right now we have six kids that are going to school that are sponsored by the NARWA Group. Every year we contribute around 70,000 shillings. Some of the money is used to help those who want to start a business. We monitor each other's progress each year. We even go so far as punishing one that is not doing right.

What motivated my uncle and me to begin this group is the kind of lives people are living in the family. They come from a humble background. But I realize we have the power to do something. If we can just motivate them then they can see the light. So far we have one family member, Kennedy Wafula, who was in secondary school when we began the project. Now, through attending our meetings and working hard, he finished university last year and is a high school teacher. Now it is his turn to help three kids to go to school.

NARWA started with relatives but now it has expanded to many youth in the village. It has a membership of 70 committed people. We contribute money towards one pool so that in future we will be working like a cooperative bank, giving loans and helping our group members. Every December I teach about how to survive in a hard economic situation like Kenya.

I have also formed a reach-out ministry called ROTJIM (Reach

Out Team for Jesus International Ministry). Though it is feeble now, in the future it is going to be a big organization in Africa. Our aim is to reach all the youth in the remote villages; to empower them by knowledge of the word of God and provide knowledge on how to help them improve themselves economically. We go around discouraging outdated traditional practices like female genital mutilation (FGM) that is practiced in many parts of Africa. We teach about HIV/AIDS and general cleanliness. We discourage idleness and encourage youth to be creative and to engage in income generating activities instead of waiting for government employment that is not easily found. I do mission work in different part of Kenya and Africa. Because of what I have passed through in life, I am able to tell them others that it is possible to come out of bad situations, even if there seems to be no way.

Two of my sisters are HIV positive; I always feel for them and many other young girls from this cult that are suffering the same disease. Our vision as ROTIM is to teach and enlighten the girls about the dangers of HIV/Aids. In the future, if this goes well, I will focus on helping young girls in the village who are already engaged in illicit activity because of poverty. One of my sisters has such a story. She got Aids because she was working as a household helper in Nyanza and her boss is the one that transmitted Aids to her. I do feel the helplessness of young ladies who are working in such jobs and long to help them.

My story is not finished. It has only begun. There is so much I want to do with God's help.

(At this writing Nic is married to Hellen Wasika and they now have a daughter, Tabitha. Nic has pioneered Certificate of Ministerial Training for Mt. Elgon. Twenty two pastors and lay leaders graduated in his first batch. A second batch is hard at work completing the course.)

A BIT OF A FOOL
Gezahegn Amare

Though I was born in an Orthodox Christian family that gave little attention to religion, I had the desire to know and serve God from the time I was six years old. In 1978 I got registered at an Orthodox church to be a Sunday School Choir member by paying fifty cents. During the eight years I stayed in that church I was on the verge of becoming a highly devoted kind of monk. Because of this, my friends used to tease me and give me a nickname *Sholawsholiti* which means "a little religious person who is a bit of a fool." The word *sholaw* is the name of a tree from which everyone just takes whatever they want. Monks were often like that, people thought.

When I was 14 years old, I, by the guidance and help of the Lord, read the Bible from Genesis to Revelation and started to devotedly serve the Lord. It came about in this way. On September 11, 1981, the Archbishop of the Ethiopian Orthodox Church visited our church for a special occasion. I presented an oration on the doctrine of the Trinity. As a reward His Holiness gave me a Bible. Though it is not that way now, at that time for me to have a Bible was a very unusual thing and a great privilege because only priests had Bibles. From that same day I began to read the Bible. I read for at least one hour in Amharic every day. I really didn't understand what I was reading. My goal was just to finish it. However, I must have digested something because after I read for one year I started to question the traditions of my church. I questioned the kissing of the gate and bowing when they entered the sanctuary compound. I asked myself, "Why are we doing these things? I can't find them in the Bible." I asked priests but they didn't seem to have an answer for me.

For two years this continued until one day I became very disappointed with an Orthodox priest. The year was 1985. I realize not all priests were like this one, but I had such an idealistic faith that one bad apple spoiled the whole bucket for me. It was on a very special day in July when children were allowed to take holy communion and so there were other young boys around. I had gone to my very special place of prayer which was hidden from the view of everyone. To my shock and horror this priest was using that place to defile the "temple." I was angry and shocked and totally dismayed. I expected that when this priest would go into the sanctuary that like Arius who denied Christ by teaching that there was a time when Jesus did not exist, his chest would burst open and he would die. But God didn't judge him and the priest acted like everything was normal.

Because of his audacity I fled from the church, shouting like a mad man. The priests apprehended me and baptized me in holy water because I was shaking with anger, asking, "God where are you?" They thought I was crazy. They beat me with crosses trying to cast out my demon. For twenty-one days this continued. Then they left me alone. By that time my interest in any religion had died. We were studying Marxism and Leninism in school, so it was easy for me to find people who didn't believe in God. I began to collaborate with a communist political teacher. We began a campaign against religion and against having faith in God. We made this campaign at schools and district communist meetings. In these district communist gatherings I testified against religious ministers who lived contrary to what they preached. I also started to teach my peers about Marxism and Leninism. That lasted for about two years. But the Lord did not want me to continue in this activity.

In 1988 I came into conflict with some people. I was a martial arts fan and was keen to practice on people. However, only soldiers were allowed to study these military techniques, so I had to learn in secret. After I thought I had learned a technique I wanted to try it out on someone who knew that technique, of necessity, a soldier. One day, I went to a bar to find someone to fight. At this time there were many soldiers in Addis Abba. Many of them were among people roasting maize on the roadside. I didn't know I needed to respect the marks of rank on a soldier's shoulders so I tried to challenge one of them. The soldier thought I was just a small kid of 16 and was not prepared for my fast kick. I quickly beat him with my leg and he fell into the maize's charcoal fire. Everyone wanted to attack me so they started to chase me. While I was running away from them I became tired. I turned to the left and entered a certain compound. The place I entered happened to be a protestant church called "Bethel MekaneYesus." (Bethel Lutheran/Presbyterian Church. The Lutherans and Presbyterians had become one to strengthen each other when the Communists took over).

I entered the church hall and sat down. There were a lot of people inside. At that time the preacher was preaching about enmity between people. Because of sin, he said, man becomes the enemy of God, of himself and his neighbors and even of his own nature. Enmity becomes our nature. I started to think, "This place I think is good. I need to hear this again." The day was Friday and I determined to come again on Sunday. It was almost Easter time, the end of April. After this I went every Friday and Sunday to that church because I enjoyed listening, but I still didn't believe there was a God.

Six months later they announced a conference. I didn't know what that was. On that day I came late and because the church was really full I couldn't get inside. At this time all the Pentecostal and Baptist churches had been closed by the communists. Only those denominations which were considered close to Orthodoxy in theology were allowed to operate. So, every believer would go to these churches and the Orthodox allowed these churches to have separate meetings in their facilities. The Presbyterians were in charge of this conference but all of the other groups had come, too, so there was no place even in this big compound for me to sit. I waited until lunch break.

When people went out for the two-hour lunch break I managed to enter the sanctuary. I went to the very first row of benches. I sat there looking at the altar which had a cross and Bible on it with candles on both sides. As I focused on the altar a cloud arose from the Bible. I could scarcely believe my eyes. It moved up to the roof and became really thick. As I watched it came back down and beat me on the head. Heavy fear entered my heart. I thought I would go to hell. I said, "How do I dare to say there is no God? What a sinner I am." I began to weep. When the conference started, I didn't hear anything – neither what the preacher said, nor what the singers sang. I just continued to weep. Even when I went home I was still weeping to the point that my mom thought I had lost my mind again. That terrible shaking lasted for three days. I neither ate nor slept. After three days I took the Bible that His Holiness had given me and I stood holding it, saying, "God I know you are real. From now on I will live for you. If I get a chance I will die for you." This is how I confessed my sin and received Jesus

Christ. I could never be a stranger in the house of the Lord after that. From the very first service I attended after my awakening, I helped arrange chairs and whatever that I saw needed to be done, I did. I used to ask questions about things I did not understand and I immediately started to evangelize outside the church. When the people I evangelized asked me questions about things I did not know I brought them to church and connected them with ministers who could answer their questions.

My evangelizing took me from shop to shop and home to home. At this time the Communists were still in control of the government but because there was fighting everywhere: they were losing control. All of the young men were being taken to be in the army. Everyone was afraid but because the communists told them there was no God they were especially afraid because they didn't know they could have a God in whom they could trust. This context gave me an advantage. I started to preach the existence of God everywhere I went and people started to respond to me and they accepted Jesus. I brought them to church and a lot of people in my town received Him. Some of them wanted to be my friends because when they heard me they were really encouraged. I always had gatherings in my home as a young man but then the Lutheran/Presbyterian church started to question me because there were more than one hundred people following me. When I preached and prophesied many people came. The Lutherans were asking me if this was a church? "No, the church is there." They thought I was preaching heresy because planting a new church was unheard of. In fact, it was not legal. There were many people attending my meetings from the Lutheran/Presbyterian Church, Catholics and even Muslims. Sometimes I would preach all day in a believer's home. One group would come, go, and another would come.

After two years the government changed and democracy was announced. The closed churches re-opened. At that time I found the Full Gospel Church. I joined there with my more than 120 followers. I baptized everyone who was following me by immersion. We would go to someone's bathroom and baptize people. In the Lutheran/Presbyterian church I was just a member, but here I was the first catechism teacher. My teaching was very effective with new believers. For two years every month more than 100 people were baptized. I would tell them, "If you really want to be a Christian, you must be a witness." I will teach you and within 3 weeks we will finish the class. When you bring two other students, you will be baptized. It was such an exciting time.

After two years, another conflict came. There was a man that I really loved. He is probably my second hero. The first would have been the man who preached to me first in the Presbyterian church, a very prayerful man. The second man was really bold and he had been imprisoned many times. (I myself was imprisoned two times during communist times and five times during democracy.) His name was Apostle Zewde. He is now in England. He brought boldness into my heart. When I saw him I felt zeal grow there. The way he preached was like a warrior and strengthened me so much to be a warrior, too. This man was such a model of Christ to me.

However, he wanted to start a new denomination and I was against that. By then, since the communist times ended we were really expanding – millions were coming to Christ, but there were no new denominations. Before Zewde, we were devoted to the Lutheran/Presbyterian church. But now we had followed Zewde to the Full Gospel Church. Since the Communist government was gone great revival was everywhere. Zewde wanted to start his own denomination called Rhema Faith according to Kenneth Hagen's teachings. I didn't really want to join him. I loved him and appreciated him, except that starting a new church I looked on as being bad behavior. I argued with him, but he said God told him to start a new church and he went.

After he went out from the Full Gospel one of the Full Gospel big ministers started to think that I was Zewde's follower so they didn't need me there with them anymore. Furthermore, they wanted to denounce Zewde. When they said Zewde was a heretic, I thought, "Maybe he has made mistakes but he is not a heretic." They didn't want me to stay in the Full Gospel church anymore because I wouldn't speak against Zewde. Until now I still don't speak against him. I really love him. I really loved the Full Gospel church, too. So, I didn't join him in his church but neither did I stay in Full Gospel. I stayed in the middle and I prayed a lot and finally God directed me to the Gospel Deliverance Church.

The Deliverance Church trained me in Bible School and gave me a diploma. Up to this point I was planting churches near Addis Ababa. Now I began to travel further. They gave me 250 Ethiopian biir (about 1250 ksh/$12.50 per month). Of this, I sent my future wife 150 biir per month and I remained with only 100. For five days during this church planting season I ate the stalks of the maize plant. That did not hinder me from planting 7 churches. All of these were among the Muslims. It wasn't easy though. One of these churches was called "Jel-lo-di-dah" in a tribe called Aracy. They were 100% Muslim.

After I had spent much time without winning a single soul, one day I saw an old man who was carrying a heavy burden of food. As he had passed me, the Holy Spirit told me to help him. I went and asked him if I could carry his load. I walked 20 kilometers carrying that load – a 3½ hours walk. When we arrived at his home, I rested. They gave me food and asked me many questions, "Why do you want to help us?" I said that it was Allah who sent me there. I want to tell you about Nabilsah." Then I told them about Jesus. They really loved it. They brought their relatives and all the children. In that place there was no mosque.

From that day on, I would go to their place in the morning to teach them and at night I would return to the town. They started to understand and devote their lives to Jesus. After two or three months I had almost concluded my catechism class. Then I made one mistake. In town there was an Ethiopian Orthodox Church where I had started to preach. When they refused to listen to me, I said, "You have the Bible, Jesus and the cross but you shut your hearts to Jesus and you will go to hell. But these Muslims have opened their hearts to Jesus and they will go to heaven." Before I could go back to visit the Muslims, they had sent someone to the Muslims to tell them that I was mocking the Muslims and talking against them. When those who had really trusted me heard this word, they became annoyed. You see, if they think someone is against them, the best thing they can do is kill them. They told their young men that when I would come there, they would not sleep and they would prepare their dogs against me, too. I was running to visit the former Muslims one morning. After I had traveled about two hours, my heart started to think bad things, so I started to sing a song about the devotion of Moses, "May my place be with the

Lord. I will run until my old age. If I don't find anyone to bury me, my soul will go to heaven." When I was about to reach their compound – about 250 meters from the gate--I saw them standing outside. The last time I had come they were waiting for me inside singing, but this time they were outside with their dogs and spears and they looked at me like a criminal. My heart started to pound. I was thinking, "Can I go back home?" But something in my spirit said, "No, it is good to go to them. If I die it is a blessing while I am preaching." So I went. When I had gone almost 50 meters, I saw a big, black angel – like a mountain. It covered the whole land. He had big muscles and he opened a huge scroll. The scroll said, "Nothing by any means shall harm you." My body was afraid but I had a kind of confidence inside. When I came near the village, they started to run to me. The older guy said, "Children stay, let him come." The dogs were barking against me and they said, "What bad thing have we said about you?" I said, "Nothing." "Why are you mocking our people with the Orthodox people?" I replied, "In my religion, mocking someone is *haram* (forbidden). You gave me food, you gave me your milk and you were always protecting me. How could I speak against you?" This old man said, "Now, these Ethiopian Orthodox people are really shrewd. They want to make enmity between us and you. Do what you want to do. You wanted us to be baptized. Now, do it! From now on I will stop chewing tobacco and you can have some land here to build a church." I baptized almost 39 members of that family: 1 husband, 5 wives and 17 children and a lot of grandchildren. They gave me eucalyptus trees. We cut them up and started to build a church while I continued to teach them. That church is now a big Full Gospel church. That is one great thing that God did for me before I married. After that there were six more churches planted among their relatives.

Before I married I had planted 3 churches for Full Gospel and 7 churches for Deliverance. I returned from the field after one and a half years of church planting with the Deliverance Church to prepare for my wedding. When they saw me come the Deliverance Church leaders were annoyed. "Who is taking care of the churches?" "I only came for one month to prepare my wedding. I have not spent a lot of time." This brought conflict. I was very hurt. I had arranged a very simple wedding. The expenses had amazingly been provided by high school students. My wife and I had been leaders in the Christian movement in high school and everyone knew us. When we came to be married they all gathered together to help us. They made everything for us and invited about 350 people. My church didn't do anything because they resented the timing of the marriage and thus didn't support me.

My plan was to marry and to take my wife immediately with me for church planting, but when we didn't agree with the church I decided I'd stay in Addis Ababa for one month with my wife. In Addis my mom refused to give me a room with my wife. When she saw what the students had done – bought an ox, prepared a buffet, gathered 35 cards - my mom, my sister and my brother all thought that I had a lot of money and they refused to help me. The place I had to take my wife was really small and awful, but there was one big house that the Redemption Church (from Nigeria) had for church planting. It was a really smart house and it was empty. One of my best men knew them and told them about me, so they gave me the big compound. They said, "Gezahegn always preaches, so let him sleep here and preach." Therefore, my honeymoon was in a big compound, but without any furniture.

Sunday after our wedding we went to that compound and we had a great revival while still in our gowns and at 11pm in the night we were still preaching and celebrating and praying. Most people say that Gezahegn is really good in preaching and prayer but he doesn't know how to put the brakes on. There is no stopping. We gave an announcement that the following Wednesday that we would have overnight prayer. The first Wednesday there were about 32 people and the second Wednesday there were a hundred. When my Deliverance Church saw this, they thought, "Gezahegn is going to that church, we won't use him in planting churches, but let us have him here in his own house." They told me, "You need to have your own home. Go out from the Redemption Church. You can preach in your own house." They rented a house and gave me permission to preach from there. Compared to my Mom's house it was very good. I called it Deliverance Bible School. There was a program from 9 to 11, 1 to 3 and 5 to 7. A lot of people came to learn. The subjects were Evangelism, Prayer, and Healing. People came from many denominations. For 10 months

I stayed there and it was great. Sometimes the students would collect money and give it to me. So I told the church they didn't have to pay the rent, because the students would pay. However, a new administration came in the church and they asked me to stop teaching in my home. I had to minister in church. I went to church but they told me I didn't have to work every day. I needed to preach only Wednesday and Sunday. That was boring for me. Each service was 2 hours only.

Life became very difficult. There was a crisis every time; we argued and always gathered and discussed my program. Finally I said, "From September, I don't want money from you. I won't work for the church. I will preach everywhere I want and I will support my family doing some business." I started to make soap and within 3 to 5 days, I started to make money. Within 2 days I would get my whole month's salary by making soap. I started to preach everywhere and people started to come. But Pastor Melaku, a pastor of Deliverance Church came to my home and said, "You don't have to work. It will be a curse for you." "No, I told him. I'll not work for the church from now on. Why? Because always we argue with each other." He said, "Ok. You may be disappointed with our church. Go to another church." "No, Satan will go there, too. I've been in the Lutheran Church, Full Gospel Church, Deliverance Church," and I know Satan would be there, too."

But Pastor Melaku told me about Pastor Hirui and his devotion to the ministry. Then I thought, "I want to be with this man." When Pastor Melaku introduced us, Pastor Hirui asked me "What do you want to do in ministry?" "I don't want to join any ministry, I want to plant a church." He said, "You can." He told me to find a hall in the town and go plant a church. That is how I started to work with the Church of God. Pastor Melaku was protecting me. The church had thought I should just work one day a week. A carpenter spends 40 hours of work in his work. I needed to do the same."We will rent you a house and we will give you a microphone," and that very week I rented a house and started to preach. After six months 25 people were baptized. That was 17 years ago. I planted this church and it grew and grew. The things I feared came. When my converts grew they started to question me. Especially a man named Ayechiluhem. When they made conflict I asked Hirui to be my successor, appointed him as pastor and left there. Now the church has 300 members. One of the girls made an album and is a famous singer. Her baby brother is now grown up and singing with her.

Then I went to another place where my mission was to plant a church for Somalis. I labored about 2 years without any result. After 2 years 7 people responded and I started a fellowship.

Because I didn't have a place, I gathered them in my bishop's house. One of them stole something so I had to stop meeting there and went to another place where I started another church. Within one year there were about 72 young people. We had a kind of repentance class, discipleship 1, discipleship 2, and discipleship 3. Repentance class would play football or do drama or have an English class. Discipleship 1 was Bible School. My converts started to grow. I had one who used to follow me. Her name was Meron. When the church started, she became a really good singer. She knew the rhythms which I don't know, though I loved to sing. But she knew how to sing really well. I gave the church to her so she became a pastor and I went to the countryside with the Church of God. That was 10 years ago. Meron was my friend and my follower. She liked everything that I did and became a good pastor herself.

One time a Latino pastor from the Church of God came. He visited the place and encouraged us and I gave myself to planting churches in Sellale in two towns. After 6 months the calling from everywhere to start churches came to us. Demons were cast out and people received healing. Everyone liked my preaching. It was kind of new for me. 25 churches were planted in three years. We passed to a place called Gindebert and another 15 churches were planted. That year was really blessed. We were focusing on the south before but now we started to go north. We were called everywhere to start churches. I was responsible to arrange meetings, appoint pastors everywhere, teach and preach. In the middle of this though I was happy. But by this time I had 3 children, and my family started to starve. My wife started to question me, too. Yes, I had success outside but my family was starving at home. I was happy but my monthly salary was not enough even for one week.

Now in Ethiopia in September we have a 13th month. This month is only 5 days instead of 30 days and once in four years it becomes 6 days. Our tradition is that that particular month is for fasting. If I had questions I would shelve them until that time. When that month came I prayed to the Lord. "You gave me all these people – more than 10,000 people have been saved, but I am about to lose my family. If my wife continues like this and my family breaks up all your work will be nothing." I was weeping but God came and told me, "Take 2 street children into your home and be like a father to them." I cried, "In the name of Jesus! This is demonic. Two small boys? How can I feed another?" God spoke only once. He didn't explain. He didn't tell me anything.

For 5 days I cried for the solution but there was no other answer. Now, I am not a prophet but when I hear from the Lord I know it. I'm really confident. September 11 is our New Year. I came home and told my wife," God told me to bring 2 street children into the house." She laughed and said, "Always people told me Gezahegn was crazy – now I believe them." But she listened to me and she said, "Let us open our home. If we fail, we fail. It is better to not disobey." We started to speak to others about this. Everyone said, "Gezahegn wants to start a new thing – an orphanage by himself. Everyone mocked me, even my bishop, but my wife said, "If you want to start this, let us save some money." In September we had saved 20% from our food money. In October and November we saved 20%. By November, I felt I'd disobeyed, that I'd not obeyed God to bring them. I told my wife, "I have to bring them now." "We don't have enough money," she replied."I don't care," I said.

We went to find two street boys. There are 80,000 street children in Addis Ababa. "Which is the one I should pick?" God gave me wisdom that I was to take two. He told me to go outside and start to play football by myself. The street children came. "Do you want to play? There is a law. We will play for 2 hours, anyone who curses his friend's mother, he will go." I don't know how I was doing this. I just did it. Within 30 minutes everyone cursed someone's mother. It was like music in their mouths. I took them to the church to take a shower. I gave them a loaf of bread. "Next Thursday come and we will play but keep your mouth. If someone curses, again I will end you out." Eight of them didn't curse. I couldn't choose from 8. I wanted two only but I didn't have any other qualifications. So I said, "Let them come and sleep in my room." Under my wife's bed I made one mattress for eight of them. They fought every night almost all the night. My wife said, "Oh Gezahegn, you are about to kill me." The struggle was hard. The first problem was our crowded quarters. Money became the second problem. But, when the boys started to reconcile with their parents, through them God gave me another vision. They began to say, 'If I'm living like this, I can go home. There is more peace in my own home.'" So they started to reconcile with their families. I know that is why God had me take the children into my home.

Now the vision changed to reconciling. Within two years 66 children were reconciled with their families. The money came and went. My family started to eat. Money was no longer a problem for me. I even started to give the first fruits to my church – not a tithe – but what was fully given to the church. Someone would come and give me something. I would spend it and more money came. Until this time 274 children have been reconciled with their families. 181 children have been trained in different kinds of work and 25 children are living in our care – 10 of them in our home. 15 of them live in two small shelters nearby.

But, I wanted to study. I was offered a chance to study at our seminary in India. I told everyone I was going. Their policy was for me to take the whole family there. But the Indian government refused to give me a visa. After they refused, about a year later, I was accepted to come to Discipleship College. They also said, "Come with your family," but I said, "If I go there I have to take all the street children with me," so my wife and I discussed it and she agreed to be the manager of that ministry. "How could I continue it while studying?" I wondered. God gave me 3 words of wisdom – principles or methods to continue. 1. When I would go home for Christmas I should arrange a Christmas tournament for all the street children in the town according to police records according to the street where they are sleeping. Each area was to arrange a football team and we would have a competition. We would make them take a shower, tell them to be reconciled, and give them an opportunity to work. 2. Because the girls were not interested in football, God gave me another vision to reach them. We did drama, singing and worship and the street girls

liked it. Another church helped for just that program. Last Christmas their gathering was held at Teacher's Association Hall, not in a church.
3. Before last Christmas I worked at Discipleship to get money and I saved it. I was about to invest about 30,000 Ethiopian biir – about $1800 -- but God blessed it and multiplied it even more.

When I had spent 80,000 biir – we had Giving the Flavor of Education for street children. This time a medical doctor taught them as a science teacher. There were engineers, journalists, artists, and national football players who came and cooperated with me. We encouraged street kids and they reconciled with their families. And some of them started to work with us. Now it has become everybody's ministry and others have started to work and think and pray about it. The next vision will be a camp and after five years a university. Maybe I will not be the leader; someone may take over. I have changed the name now because of this vision. I've changed from Mordecai Life Changing Sports Ministry to Messiah's Redemption Mission: The Savior of the World. When I go home I will have an Esther ministry called Esther Beauty for Holiness ministry with beauty salons, etc. This will be one part of the camp. Some will do life skills work as well as spiritual things. Now we will have 3 or 4 programs – Mordecai, Ester, Family of Faith (special concern for Christian families, like this year, giving shoes for evangelist's children). It is all part of Messiah's Redemption Mission. Redemption is a shade which covers everything. The program Mordecai will be one program within the vision. There will be other programs under it. It is based on the verse, "Rescue those who are being taken away to death." Proverbs 24:11. My vision is big but I know God will make it happen. To him be the glory!

Tea Without Sugar: Chastened for a Destiny

DEADLY DIAGNOSIS

Petronilla Mbakaya

While growing up, in upper primary, I developed a strong desire to serve God. I purposed to go to the convent to join the sisterhood, being of a Catholic background. Because I was very religious, I was also greatly influenced by an aunt to become part of a group called Lego Maria. It is actually a cult. I was very close to this aunt and spent most of my holidays with her. Because of this aunt's influence, I gradually lost interest in the convent. In the Quaker high school I attended, I was introduced to the salvation dimension but I never understood it. I continued going back to the Lego Maria sect even after high school. I obtained a second division mark in O levels exams but couldn't proceed to A level because my father was not very stable financially and he had other children to educate.

By chance I got a job in the Nakuru municipality and began teaching in primary school from 1985 to 1987. At that time I was admitted to Egerton University College where I pursued a diploma in agriculture and home economics which I completed in 1990. By then the government was looking for teachers so I was offered a job by TSC to teach as a UT (Untrained Teacher). My first posting was Wayway Secondary School, Sigor, West Pokot. I continued teaching there from October, 1990, to May, 1992, when I joined Kenya Technical Teacher's College to pursue a diploma in technical education.

Tea Without Sugar: Chastened for a Destiny

Deadly Diagnosis

One week-end, while at KTTC, some brethren were doing door-to-door evangelism. They shared Good News I had never heard before. I asked them many questions, and they answered them all. When they asked me to receive Jesus Christ, I received Him. That night I could not sleep. I was convicted so much; I left my bed, knelt down, and invited Jesus Christ into my life once more, on my own. The next move I made was to go to fellowship, which I had avoided because I was shy to stand before people. Meanwhile, I continued with the Catholic Fellowship. One of the brothers who had come to witness to me, sent another brother to me. At this time I was in relationship, getting ready for marriage. I remember the brother asking, "Have you considered being married to a brother?" I dismissed his suggestion by telling him, "Any man can be good, whether a brother or not." But, somehow along the line I got convicted so I called my fiancé to tell him that I was saved and wanted to change my mind about marriage. He said salvation was a good choice, but I shouldn't change my decision, but should continue our relationship. Thus, we continued, I went home to meet his parents and

We planned for our wedding in December, 1992. During the occasion, in the speeches, many encouraged us to put God first. This statement was repeated by so many, that it stood out for both of us until we had no choice but to get serious with God in our new family.

Initially, we used to go to a branch of the church where we were wed in Mombasa. It was far from where we were staying, and going there became costly. Every Sunday we went to this church, but were not blessed because they preached in the Luo Language. At the end of every service they would raise money. It became like a routine. This trend upset my husband, so we stopped going to the church.

Back at home our family decided that we must make a change and go to another church. Finally, we settled on the church in our neighborhood, which was called Likoni Christian Church, KAG (Kenyan Assemblies of God) church. The pastor was our neighbor. We were received well and my husband introduced me to the elders of the church. We were happy in the church. The happiest moment in the church was when I got my first-born twins, Justin and Christabel. The women's fellowship helped us with lots of presents. We felt good; the children grew and joined the Sunday school. During their first two years, the twins used to fall sick and many times I was hospitalized. There was a woman in the church who encouraged me to pray, pleading the blood of Jesus. She also urged me to give my tithe. It was not easy, but I began paying my tithe. I was recognized as a member of that church.

One Christmas holidays I traveled down country to Kakamega to visit my parents. On Sunday I decided to go for service at a nearby church at Khayega Market. I met a guest preacher who was preaching without looking at a Bible. I was surprised because I could follow him word for word in my Bible. This man was Harrison Oulo. His message on that Sunday was focusing on "The Appointed Time of the Lord" from the book of Genesis (21:2). He stressed that Abraham believed God until at the appointed time he and Sarah got a baby. He exhorted everyone to believe God for anything.

By then I was facing challenges in my marriage, and I was desiring that my husband might get saved. He used to drink every day, though on Sundays we would go to church. Most Sundays he looked for excuses for not going to church. At the end of that service, I reached for that scripture. I greeting Brother Harrison and requested him to come to our church in Mombasa. He accepted and asked me to go and arrange with my pastor.

When I went back to Mombasa, I told the pastor but he did not accept immediately, so it became a prayer item until he gave me the dates. I communicated with Pastor Harrison who agreed to come to our church. When he came, his first message was "The Most Important Power in the Universe," which was the power of the resurrection. People were blessed by his visit, so they invited him to come another time with his wife. He stayed in our house and we prayed together. When he traveled home to Kakamega he stopped to visit at Matsu Girls where his wife was a teacher. Slowly by slowly, my husband began to change. Once he invited the pastor and elders to our house for supper and then he gave his life to Christ. We really thanked God. But, all of sudden he started to fall sick. His skin had reactions, and especially his face. He was treated by several doctors, until he was referred to a skin doctor in Nairobi, Dr. Waweru. Dr. Waweru examined him and found him to be HIV positive. That was 1997 but my husband didn't reveal the bad news to me. However, I also started falling sick. I would be fine one day, sick the next. I was hospitalized on several occasions, often with malaria. Suddenly it was dis-covered that I was also expecting another child. I just thanked God.

One day I checked my husband's briefcase and found a letter addressed to my name, saying that I should go to Mombasa hospital for an Elisa test. I didn't know what it was until one day I was reading a newspaper. Elisa test is a test for HIV. I almost lost my breath. I called on God to help me. I started to recall my husband's salvation experience. I then realized this was the driving force behind his conversion. I just thanked God for everything. It then happened that one of his cousins was marrying in Nairobi so we were traveling to Nairobi. When we reached there he insisted we go to Afia Center for some lab tests. So they took my blood and said the results would be out in two weeks time. After the wedding we traveled back to Mombasa.

After two weeks I started asking my husband for the results and he said we would go back to Nairobi to get them. When he came back he didn't want to tell me the results, but I questioned him and finally he told me that my blood had a problem and that I needed to take some medicine called AZT to prevent the baby from being infected. So I used the drug. I got my baby through Caesarian, but the wound refused to heal. This made me go to the hospital and I stayed there for a month. (It was during the first strike of nurses from November to December of 1997). Dr. Waweru had written a letter to the doctor concerning me, instructing how the baby should be handled. I regret to say I didn't like how the Christian nurses treated me in the hospital, but I remember one Muslim nurse who took time to talk with me. I don't hold a grudge but I was disappointed.

Up until that time no one had known about my condition except one teacher who stood with me. In fact she's the one who took me to the hospital, and stayed at my side. She went to call my husband to get a signature for me to go to the operating theatre. God bless her.

I remember the moment when I came out of the anesthesia. It seems I had been in a nice place. It was very clean; there was a lot of light blue color which was very cool. There was one attendant. Maybe it was an angel. When I came to my senses, I was worshipping God with a loud voice, thanking Him. Many people had come to my bedside, watching. Suddenly I was being told, "Here is your baby." I saw a tiny, small girl. I gave her the name, Annie Praise Muali, after my mother. I thought that I wouldn't get another baby, so that she would be a remembrance of my mother to the next generation.

The church stood with me and the elders came and made a prayer of faith with me. However, my health deteriorated and they thought I was dying. I remember our pastor visited me in the house. I felt I was going. I was losing my breath and saying, "Pastor Songa, I'm dying." He rebuked the spirit of death, declaring that I would live. I was once again rushed to the hospital, but the baby remained at home. I stayed for another week in the hospital and then I was released to go home.

That December, 1997 when we approached Christmas, I was still weak. Revival was planned in the church, which was to go into the New Year. Our preacher had invited Pastor Harrison to come to the church again for a revival service. He and his wife were staying with another family, but they would come and pick me and take me to the revival meetings. After the revival meetings, they moved to our house and they stayed with us for a while. They prayed for me, counseled and encouraged me and did all they could for me.

Once we had gone to Nairobi to visit Dr. Waweru so he could examine the baby and me. We were examined in the laboratory in Hurlingham. The doctor said he would communicate the results to us. After some time, the report showed that the baby and I were negative, but my husband was positive. This report encouraged me to continue to learn and advance in my studies.

We could not continue on with this doctor, however, because it was very expensive. We could not afford to buy drugs from this doctor. At that time HIV/AIDS medication was being sold. At a later time my husband was put on the AMPATH program at Moi Referral where he got free medicine. I was examined also with the baby and we were found to be negative.

My husband was then transferred to Eldoret. Harrison and his wife prayed and suggested another pastor friend of theirs, Reverend Likavo, in Eldoret. They told me to look for his church when I arrived in town. We found a house in an area called West Indies near the church called Christian Growth Center. I got to know the pastor and his wife. It was strange to them that I was the only HIV positive person in that town whom they knew. We got along well, raised money, and purchased land for that church, so that the church could move to a new site.

After some time we moved from those houses and went to stay in Mwanzo neighborhood. Eldoret was very near our home, Naitiri, where we had bought a farm. Now that we lived in Eldoret I could go home to the farm often. These visits made me feel at home, not like when I was in Mombasa.

It was at this time that I learned about my husband's immoral behavior. Neighbors would report to me what was happening, how he would bring women to the house. There was one common law wife, called Nancy, who stayed at the market. This one he had met in Mombasa, in fact she had been my student in Mombasa. She had even come to visit me in our house. I did not know my husband and she had become intimate. Often when she was doing business at the market, she would come to our home when I was away at school. I came to know many other affairs and this became very painful to me.

When I moved to Eldoret, I commuted to a school to teach called Kapkoiga Girls. Then, due to the balancing of teachers, I was transferred to another school, which was even further, called St Paul's Makongi. It was far more costly. My husband struggled to get me other schools through some of his friends and finally managed to get me two schools: Mwiruti or Paul Boit Boy's, but I chose Mwiruti because there was a lady in charge of teachers there who was very friendly to me.

Spiritually, I was still unstable, crying to God all the time, blaming my husband. I often wanted to be in the company of this sister who was in charge of the teachers. I would pray with her every day at lunch time. We "raised an altar to God" and starting praying about furthering our education. I left Mwiruti in 2000 I continued to seek God, but would often fall sick. Sometime in 2004 I was tested again. At that point they said I was positive and they registered me in the program at AMPATH and started me on TB prevention drugs. At that time Anne Praise was still negative. I was told my CD4* was okay and I continued on with life. I never fell sick. If I did, I was given antibiotics and I felt better. I continued to serve God. He gave me mercy and love.

Someone suggested to me to attend Moi University but I was not financially stable. My husband refused because he had taken some loans and he felt we did not have enough money. We were really depending on my salary. My teacher friend, Claire Muhuha, made time and came to Discipleship University and inquired about finding some course to do there. She had a degree already from Baraton University. Brother Gordon Bloodworth briefed her about the degree courses through Lee University.

She brought me the brochure and I decided to visit Discipleship College. I found Brother Gordon, explained my case clearly, and I thought he could not admit me because I was HIV/Aids positive and would die any time. I was not on medication. It had been stopped after delivery of my baby. But he admitted me. I arranged with my head teacher that I would be teaching only in the afternoon. I began my studies at Discipleship College. I had a big desire to be grounded in the things of God, after which I would be in a better position to serve Him. I sat in classes under the teachings of Brother Gordon, Neil Lawrence and others. They shared their lives. Their teachings touched me and changed me.

One special course at Discipleship University was on Spiritual Formation. In this course, I was asked to keep a journal in which I was writing every day. This changed my life. At times I would ask myself, "Why am I disturbing myself." Financially, I was straining. I used to walk from Mwanzo, through West Indies, across the river, through Pioneer to Discipleship, attend my classes, and then walk 3 kilometers away to the school where I was a teacher. In the evening I would walk again 4 to 5 kilometers to my house. So in all I was walking 10 kilometers each day. But I gave thanks to God. Through this I kept fit.

I continued with my studies, despite pressure in my family, especially in my marriage. My husband didn't understand what I was doing in Discipleship. But by God's grace, I pushed on. The time came when he was retrenched. He had had several disciplinary cases against him, right from Mombasa. He continued to abscond from duty. He would travel home and send information that he was sick.

He continued until the time when he was laid off. He was given his severance pay and I really thank God that he listened to my suggestion. He agreed to buy a plot in Mwanzo that I should develop. He purchased it in his name and mine and put up a foundation. He said, "The money is finished. You can continue from here." By God's grace I took a loan, and we were able to build a house. We stayed in the house without power for two years until my pay improved. I got a loan, in 2003, August. At that time my husband was hospitalized and soon passed on.

I finally graduated in 2007 with a Bachelor's Degree in Christian Ministry. I've experienced His love through people. Brother Gordon came to my financial aid until I was able to finish my studies at Discipleship. I thank God for others at Discipleship who helped me get my degree. Slowly by slowly, while at Discipleship, I began to minister to students. By the help of the Holy Spirit I continue to this day to minister to children in Sunday school, and in the neighborhood. I have continued to hold unto the ministry of prayer.

When my husband died, the family decided to walk according to tradition. I couldn't follow their traditions because they make the word of God to be of no effect. After some time they would come to the grave and make sacrifices. I told them they could do what they wanted to do, but I would not be part of it. God has never left me.

I met Pastor Gashegeshi from Emanuel Complex and shared my testimony in 2003 about my daughter, Anne Praise, who was in class one. They promised to take her and give her a bursary in their primary school in 2004. She started school there and excelled until she did her KCB in 2010 and scored 401 marks. She was selected to a join a provincial School, Lugulu Girls.

Justin did his Form Four last year and scored a B-. He went through high school by the grace of God. Christobel is doing her Form Four this year and I trust God to help her.

My CD4 count continued to be good until 2010 when it dropped to 150. I was asked to go on medication. I resisted, but finally accepted to take medicine which I would have to take for life. There was some improvement, but then the CD4 dropped again to 250. I still trust in God. He is the still the one giving me his life. I have continued steadfastly with ministry, especially in high school where I am teaching. I have faced many challenges at work, but thank God I continue to excel in my profession. Many times people think that because of my condition, I cannot perform well, but consistently my students perform better than others and they have come to acknowledge my capabilities. I have a dream of starting a noble school of excellence one day. I desire it to be a government school. Given a chance and support, I will begin a good school in Rescue Centre (a home to rehabilitate street children) that will turn out to be like Starehe in Nairobi.

I have many more experiences and I can still continue to write and write, but that is all for now.

*A CD4 count is a method used to determine the progress of an HIV/Aids positive person. CD4 cells are the lymphocytes most targeted by HIV/Aids and as the disease progresses they decrease in number.

HEAD TO TOE

Peter Mwaura Ndungu

My mother was married as the second wife in a polygamous marriage when I was age four. I never knew my real father. Leaving my grandmother's small thatched house after my mother's marriage was an unforgettable experience. She had been so kind to me and my elder sister; we missed her wonderful stories every night. She told us stories about many, many things. I can remember one, in particular. She told us that when she was the age of eight, her family was living in Eldama Ravine. She told me that one time she went to fetch firewood with her three friends. One was Kahaki, another was Jane, and the third was Waceke. The girls met four strange boys from the Kalenjin tribe. These four boys wanted to take them away. Today it would be called Kidnapping. Because she was the oldest girl, she decided to fight. She engaged herself in battle with the four boys to rescue all of the girls. She fought them until they ran away. The aim of telling us this story was to explain to us how she became one of the Mau Mau fighters. After she fought the four boys, her mother told others how brave she was. The village elders heard about it and when the Mau Mau were starting, one of the village elders introduced her to the men who were in the bush. She became one of the Mau Mau freedom fighters who fought the British until the end (The British beat them back).

Tea Without Sugar: Chastened for a Destiny

When they were in the bush, she met and married her husband, my grandfather.

Before we left grandmother's house, she gave me a gun that she had made out of timber. It didn't do anything, but I was proud of it. My joy was short-lived, however, because some bigger boys took it. I felt very bad. I tried to fight them, but I was too small. The gun was about three/fourths of a meter long. It had a shoulder strap made from the skin of an animal.

Even at a young age, I knew we were going to be living with this old man (my stepfather). Inside me, I knew that I needed a father, because I had never seen my real father. But, it was not long before my stepfather started mistreating all of us – mum, Naomi and me. He changed and became so hostile. One day I fell in his arms after a beating and I was taken to the hospital and admitted for two days. The valleys of grief became deep and wide. My mother could not help me for she was beaten, too. There was no love for her or for us, hatred dominated.

One day my mother bought me a part of shorts and a t-shirt. When my stepfather came home, he found me celebrating because I had new clothes. When he asked me who bought these new clothes, I told him it was my mother. He asked my mother where she got the money. She told him what she had done. My stepfather was a farmer and had a small hotel. My mother had taken a few eggs and sold them to get 20 shillings to buy those things for me. She knew I desperately needed clothes. I wore only a long shirt which had belonged to my father. I didn't even have trousers or shorts. But, my new clothes were totally burned by my stepfather and my mother was beaten badly for her kindness to me. It was horrible.

When my sister got sick she was not taken to the hospital. She had a kidney problem. Instead of being hospitalized, my stepfather followed the advice of an old man who told him to go and catch moles and cook them and give her soup. My sister got worse and worse. My stepfather refused treatment for my sister until my grandmother came and took her to the doctor by force. My sister had a big problem so that she could not walk straight. She developed a hump on her back. The doctors said she needed to be operated before it grew worse but my mom and my grandmother had no money, so even to this day, she can't walk straight.

When I was ten, my mother gave birth to a son who became the love of my father. However, my brother Joseph became an alcoholic, and is up to now. I only hope he will be saved before he dies. Recently, he called me and told me that he wants to be reconciled with my father. I can see that God is at work!

One time at that same young age, when my father wanted to beat my mom, I stood up to defend her. I took the piece of firewood with which he beat her because she was already down, from the beating of my stepfather. When I tried to strike him, he got me first. It was around 10 pm at night, so I had to run away from home to go back to my grandma, a distance of about six kilometers. I walked through that dark night until around 2 am when I arrived at her house. I stayed with my grandmother for about a week, at which time my mother came to look for me. I refused to go back home. Next, my step-father sent a man of his age to take me home. I refused. Finally, my grandmother gave me two cocks to convince me to go back home. She told me, "When you get home, tell your mom to cook these for you." Immediately, when I arrived home, my stepfather slaughtered the cocks and we did eat them, but I was beaten badly again.

After some years my stepfather started preparing *pombe* (local brew) and insisted that I help with those activities. Once we started making *pombe*, I could not go back to school again. In fact it was three years before I went back, this time thanks to my mother's efforts. After I finished primary level, even though I had passed to go to secondary school, my father said I couldn't go. He bought me a large *jembe* (hoe) and told me I needed to go to the shamba and work. I worked for one year and was not given a single shilling.

I ran away to live with my auntie in Nyandarua. One day I went to church with her. After the preaching, I gave my life to Jesus. I still remember the pastor, Steven Kimani. He was preaching about when Jesus was entering Jerusalem. Jesus told the disciples that "these stones you are seeing today will not be one upon the other." He emphasized that when Jesus comes, no one will cling to his relatives, instead, everyone will stand alone before God and be judged. He stressed that the time to reconcile with God was that particular moment. In my mind, I thought Jesus might be coming right then, so I surrendered my life to Him. After that, my auntie took me to a tailoring course where I trained for one year and then I went back home. By this time I was around eighteen years old.

When I went back home my father still tried to engage me in helping make *pombe*, but I refused, because now I was a Christian and I knew Christians should not do those things. It was not easy. He took a *panga* and wanted to hit me with it, but I ran away. Thank God my stepmother (the first wife of my stepfather) was a strong Christian and prayerful. She loved me and secretly taught me how to pray. Several years before, I had started attending Sunday School in the A.I.C. church. After I gave my life to Jesus, I joined forces with my stepmother. She encouraged me to stand in my salvation. Also, my mother got saved. My stepmother prayed for me and taught me about the Holy Spirit and she encouraged me to go to a Pentecostal church. That was how I joined the Full Gospel Church of Kenya. Immediately after I joined that church I was baptized with the Holy Spirit. Then my stepmother, my mom and I started praying for my stepfather. The more we prayed, the worse things became. I remember one time my father told me that if I got married I should not try to call my children by his name. I don't know how I got the courage to tell him this, but I told him, "I'll still call my children by your name." That time I stayed at home six months, helping my mother in the garden. Things finally got so bad, I had to run away. I came here to Eldoret.

When I came to Eldoret, I went to live with my uncle (brother to my mom). He arranged a job at a tanning factory for me. I worked there as a grounds man for around one year. But I wanted to work on my own. I managed to buy a sewing machine. I left the grounds job and started sewing on my own. However, in 1992, we experienced tribal clashes in Eldoret, so I could not continue my work as a tailor. During those skirmishes, I felt the call of God in my heart. I can remember the Holy Spirit telling me, "I've called you as a minister of the Gospel." I didn't know what it meant. God used a lady (who is now in my church) to help me understand. God showed her in a vision that I was sitting somewhere and near me there was a very big tent. I was trying to pull out the tent poles. An angel came from heaven and told her, "Tell Peter to not pull out those tent poles, because I have called him to the ministry. Instead of pulling them out he should stretch the tent." When this lady told me the vision, I fasted and prayed for 7 days. The Holy Spirit spoke to me very clearly that he had called me to the work of the ministry. From that time to this day I can still remember clearly what He spoke to me.

In 1993 the Holy Spirit spoke gain to me and told me to go back to Mwiruti to start a Full Gospel Church. But I had doubts. I didn't believe that I could manage to start a church, but the Holy Spirit spoke to me that night and showed me a vision. I saw many sheep lying under an acacia tree and a wolf came to attack them. When the wolf was trying to attack the sheep, I shouted, "Help!' When I said that, a shepherd's staff came from heaven and fell into my hand and I defended those sheep. Immediately after that vision, the Holy Spirit told me, "That's what I've called you to do." Immediately, I went to Mwiruti and started the church. It was a funny thing because I went there and rented a very small room, but I had no benches. For two months I was just there alone. I would go and pray the whole day and pretend I was preaching to people until one day, after I finished preaching, I met a woman whom we called Mama Wangare. She recognized me and called me by name, "Peter what are you doing here?" "I just came from the church and now I'm going back home." The Holy Spirit spoke to me to share with her the love of Christ. She accepted Jesus and agreed to come the following Sunday to church. Now I had someone to preach to. I had to lead the service, pray for the service, pray for the offering, preach, and lead the songs. But from that moment, God used that lady to talk to people. She also introduced me to her friends, who received Christ. After one year, there were 62 members and we managed to buy a church plot which cost us 20,000 ksh.

It wasn't long before I had a disagreement with my senior pastor. He decided to come and take over the church and I was left outside. So I had to find another church to work with. That's how I joined Gospel Evangelistic Church of Kenya where I pastor today.

I ministered alone for four years before I decided it was time to marry. I approached the first lady with whom I thought we could agree to marry, but she refused. I approached about five ladies who refused. I remember one of the ladies told me that she couldn't marry a poor pastor. According to me she was right. I didn't have enough cloth to sew to earn money. I couldn't pay for my house. Even food was a big problem during that time. I didn't have a bank account. I didn't have anything. So, according to me, she was right. I also remember one of the ladies, named Mercy. When I approached Mercy, she didn't say anything. She just looked at me from head to toe and then she went. I tried to follow her, but she refused to talk to me. Later on, she sent her friend to say, "Tell Peter that he should not come to me. He should go find someone that belongs to his class." My heart was very badly wounded. I decided not to marry, to remain single. I stayed for two years like that. But the desire to get married revived within me, so I decided to marry an Asian girl. I went to join a fellowship that belonged to those ladies every Thursday afternoon, just to find a girl to marry. According to Indian custom, the man does not give dowry. That was a sweet place for me. However, the Lord had other plans.

One day a pastor friend invited me to his church because he had also invited some special visitors to come and minister in his church. The lady, who is now my wife, was invited to lead praise and worship. When she was given the microphone, immediately the Holy Spirit spoke to me. "The lady with the microphone is your wife." It was such a loud voice that I thought everyone heard it. Before the meeting ended, I went outside, and I told God "If what you have spoken to me is true, I want you to create a moment now." After the meeting was over, the two of us remained in church. I'd never seen her before. I greeted her and from that moment I knew I wanted to know where she lived. I went to her place with her that very night. At least I saw the gate of where she lived with her parents! That same night she also told me where she worked. I went there and invited her to our church the following Sunday and that very day I asked her to marry me. After two days she said, "yes." She didn't look at me from head to toe. She said 'Yes!" and that's how I got married.

Many things have changed now. I went to my parents' home some years back and the same old man called me by my name, embraced me with the same hands he used to use to beat me, and this is what he said in a deep voice, "You are my son." Since he was not yet saved, he called all the people who were around and asked me to pray for him and every member of the family. Two years later he was saved.

Recently I preached in the church that he attends. He hugged me and thanked me so much for the message.

I am now experiencing the great love of a good father to a son. During Christmas last year, 2010, he called me and gave me a shamba of two acres. Love is overwhelming today in the same house where I experienced so much abuse. These are the fruits of prayer that my stepmother prayed for me. This is my third year of celebration.

When hatred dies, love, peace and inheritance kiss each other. Although hatred may dominate, the love of God will always give us great victory through salvation. No one could believe that one day I would sit with my father as a son.

The vision that I had about my ministry continues to lead and guide me. What the Lord showed me, I have obeyed. The Holy Spirit told me to go pray and fast for forty days, which I had never done before. During those 40 days, the Holy Spirit showed me a city in Germany, called Hamburg and the Lord spoke to me, "I'll send you to Hamburg," There was no specific time given, so even today I'm still waiting for that to come to pass. The Lord spoke to me that he would enlarge my ministry internationally. My associate, Pastor Kamau, was shown a vision by the Lord which he shared with me a few months ago. He was in prayer, praying to God for the ministry, asking God to direct him concerning that ministry. The Lord told him, "The reason I connected you with to Pastor Peter is for you to take care of that church and be trained. I'm going to involve Peter in ministries outside the country." I'd not shared with Pastor Kamau about my vision – so for me it was a confirmation that the Lord is preparing for me to minister in other countries.

A big part of my vision to help others is a ministry called SMOCAP. SMOCAP is an acronym for Single Mothers Caring Partners. My experience with my own mother made me realize that a single mother taking care of children without outside support is not an easy job. It gave me a burden to help others in the same situation.

One day, while going house to house doing evangelism, I met a lady named Mumbi who had three children: two sons and one daughter. When I was witnessing to her about Christ, she told me that because I had been preaching in that place for some time, everybody knew that I was a pastor. She continued to say that she believed in

Jesus, but she could not be saved because she had a secret which she could not share with anybody. I asked her what that secret was. She told me that because she could not take care of her three children, she had decided to ask the fathers of these children to help her. She told me that the father of the first child was paying school fees for the children, the father of the second child was giving food to the house, and the father of the last child was paying the house rent. In my mind I could not imagine someone living such a lifestyle. I didn't ask her how she could keep the three men, but I knew traditionally, men do not share one wife. That's why she was saying it was a secret. Because of this awful secret, she could not give her life to Jesus. She had no job, she was depending on these men to support her and her children in order for them to survive. I came out of that house shedding tears because I realized that I didn't have help to offer to that lady. I went to the church where I spent that night praying and asking God what I was supposed to do. The Lord confirmed to me that something was to be done, even though I didn't know exactly what I was supposed to do. I had failed to win Mumbe to Christ that day.*

I shared my burden with my wife. We prayed together and fasted and God gave me an idea. A question came to my mind, and I started asking myself, "What about those ladies who are already in the church—who are singles and widows?" I organized a meeting and met those ladies. I asked them to share with me their life stories, to tell me how they were living, especially how they were earning their living. They told me everything they were going through. I remember one called Teresia, a single mother of eight children, who said that even though she was in the church, many times she was tempted and prostituted herself in order to provide food for her children. Everybody in the meeting gave her own story. As we were talking, I came up with an idea. If only I could manage to give them a small amount of money to start a small business, they could earn their living without depending on men who would take advantage of their poverty. After the meeting with those ladies, I organized a fund-raising, and we managed to raise 7,000 shillings. I distributed the money to the ladies and they started small businesses like selling *sukuma wiki* (kale) and cabbages, even boiled eggs. From that time on they could continue working and supporting their families. God blessed the works of their hands. When we were buying our church plot those women gave the highest amount of money in the church, because they were working. When it came time for buying iron sheets for our building, they managed to give. In fact, Teresia gave five iron sheets, which would be the equivalent of 5,000 Kenyan shillings. To me it was great progress that they could feed their children without any problem.

However, in 2007, tragedy struck. We experienced post-election violence. Their businesses were burned down and again they had nothing. We had to start all over again. The church moved from that center to Langas where we rented a classroom at St. Elizabeth High School. Because of the skirmishes we had only a six members left. Three of them were singles, one was a widow, my wife and I. We continued fellowshipping there for about two months. After that time, God revived my vision for the singles and widows. I now had to start thinking how to get money to give to these singles and widows. I organized a fund-raising at the church and managed to raise around 12,000 ksh. After I distributed the money to them, they went to work, so they could continue to pay house rent. God really intervened in their situations. Even those who had gone to the IDP camps came back to the estates and rented houses, because they now had money to do so and were able to cater for their own food and other necessities.

After one year we shifted from the classroom to where we are worshipping now. After we shifted, the Lord spoke to me that I needed to invite other members from other churches. He spoke to me very clearly, that he wanted SMOCAP to be a blessing to many churches. From that point on, SMOCAP did not belong to Gospel Evangelical Church of Kenya only. We invited other churches' members to join SMOCAP.

Even though we started SMOCAP ministry in 2006, it was not until January, 2010 that we launched it officially. After I met Sister Waneda Brownlow, a widow, I was assisted in finding outside support for SMOCAP. We have been working together until today. We decided that every year we would be taking a group of women and last year, 2010, we had 15 to be trained in three areas: five in sewing or hair dressing, a second group raising cows and pigs, and a third group who wanted to engage in small businesses. We organized training in January and February of 2010 for those who wanted to keep animals and do business. The livestock department of the government gave me four teachers to train them in how to keep cows, pigs, chickens and rabbits. I also had one teacher train them about business. Those who were training in tailoring and hair dressing received money for training fees and we assisted them with money for food while they were training. By December 19, 2010, we organized a graduation for 9 members who had completed the training. One member was dismissed who had continued to drink alcohol, one had dropped out of hairdressing classes, and a third moved to Sudan where she had begun successfully to do business. She is now able to pay school fees for her two children. We bought a sewing machine for the lady who was taking tailoring and she is working now in that field. Those who were taking hair dressing have been employed and for those who were willing to keep animals, we managed to buy three cows for them and two pigs.

This year in January, 2011, we took another group. At this time, many people have come to know about SMOCAP so the number increased from 15 to more than 30. We divided the group again into three, as we had the previous year. We again invited teachers to do training in livestock and business. This time we had a lady who wanted to have a greenhouse so we invited also a teacher from agriculture department who came and taught about how to grow tomatoes, etc., in a greenhouse. Of the new group, five wanted to keep cows, two of them goats, and one chickens. There were five wanting to be trained— one in a hair salon, four as dress-makers. They all have completed their training now. We are only waiting to get money so that we can buy sewing machines, cows, give support for the business people and build the greenhouse for the lady who wants to do that work. We already have money to buy goats for the two ladies who want to keep goats.

When women receive money, we expect them to give a tithe back to SMOCAP and to contribute 100 shillings each month to the ministry, so that there will be money to support others. Those who get animals, we require the first offspring to be given to SMOCAP.

Our future plan is that after we have been able to assist 100 people, they will be required to contribute not less than 1000 every month, to give SMOCAP enough money to continue to be self-supporting. If any would like to buy a cow or boost a business, we could then lend her money, which she would be required to return with interest. The board members will agree about what percentage that should be. Money will be lent on the basis of their faithfulness to support SMOCAP. At this time we don't ask them to return the money that we give them, but we only ask a contribution each month as we meet. One day I believe we will have a SMOCAP guest house and training center.

The church has been very supportive in this ministry – they encourage with providing food for meetings and help in other ways. But other churches are slow to come to help. They want their members to be empowered, so if we ask how many widows and singles they have, they are very willing for us to help them, but if we want to have them give to assist the ministry, they are slow to do that. The pastors are afraid they will lose some of the money from the church. I have other ideas about how we can become self-supporting including the possibility of buying a shamba that has been offered us to grow passion fruit and a local type of beans. Another possible means of support would be starting a goat raising project in my home area. God will make a way, because He has a special love and concern for those who do not have others to help them.

*Mumbi later received Christ and is now an active member of the Full Gospel Church.

FREE BEHIND BARS
Titus Etiang

Before I was born, my grandfather had immigrated from Teso land, near Malaba, on the border of Uganda, to a village called Kaberwa, on the slopes of Mt. Elgon. After staying in Kaberwa for a few years he sold that land and went back to Teso, but my father didn't go with him.

The forest department was employing people like my father to work as foresters at a place called Kimililil. We went to stay in a village where the forest department had made an estate with houses for workers, constructed from cypress timber. Unfortunately, we couldn't notice the nice smell of the cypress, because there were so many other smells. The house was terrible. I can remember when we were young, we used to sleep on sisal sacks on the dirt floor of the house. My brothers and I would urinate at night on those sacks, making our bedding really smelly. In the morning we would hang the sacks out in the sun to dry. We couldn't afford good mattresses and bedding because our father was a drunkard. Life was almost unbearable.

The house had two rooms. My father and mother slept in one room, we children in the other. Their room was also used as the kitchen. We would go to the bush to search for firewood for cooking. I would become almost crazy thinking about how we lived.

When we woke up in the morning our father was often not there. He would wake up very early in the morning, while we were still sleeping and come back around midnight, when we were already asleep. What would awaken at that time because he started quarreling with my mom. When he fought with her, sometimes we would run away and hide at our neighbor's. Many times in the morning my mother would not cook at all because she had nothing to cook. When my father got his salary, he would often he would spend it all on liquor;

Tea Without Sugar: Chastened for a Destiny

when he came home he had nothing. Sometimes we children would go to work with my mother in some peoples' farms. We would sometimes plow (cultivate) the land, using a *jembe*. We might be given two tins of maize for our work. When we returned, we could grind the maize to make meal, which would provide food for one week – one meal each day, late at night, around 9 pm. We ate late at night so as to be able to sleep. At this time we were five: two brothers and three sisters. I was the oldest. Finally we were twelve and we are all still alive.

Life continued in that manner for some time. I went to Standard One at the neighboring school. But sometimes I remember I wore only a *kak*—a rough woolen shirt—with no shorts. That was all I had. Occasionally, when my father worked, he would bring things like a new *k kak*. My father was a well known drunkard.

After suffering like this for a long time, the forester decided to give my mother a portion of land. We went with her and my uncles who helped us to buy six bags of seeds—around 60 kilos. We had to slash and burn the bush, dig holes and put the seeds in. Mother was harsh, a real disciplinarian who reminded us of the life we were living. She would say, "I don't want you living a life like this when you grow up." That year God helped us and we had a very good harvest. I remember harvesting about 30 bags.

Mother was clever. After harvesting, she sold the bags and went outside the forest to buy land—about 1 1/2 acres. We continued to stay for another year on the estate (in the forest). Unfortunately that was the year the government told us all to leave. We had to go to the land my mom had bought and build a grass house. It was a big oval house, covered with grass, but not covered very well. Sometimes when it rained the roof leaked and we would hide in the corner. We would lie down to sleep and mother would cover us with a blanket she had made from scraps. That's how we were living in 1992 when the tribal clashes came. Our house was burned by tribes like the Bukusu. Other Teso like us were chased from Mt. Elgon. We fled to Kimilili town but there were problems because many people had fled there. We stayed without eating for 4 days.

My rich uncle and I decided to go back to the forest because we had many things back there. It was night when we sneaked back to his place. He had some animals: rabbits and chickens. We caught a rabbit—killed and roasted it. We lit a fire but hid in the bush. We had entered the place one person at a time, hoping at least one of us would survive. After we ate we went back to Kimilili.

Because life was so difficult, I began to think I might move back to Eldoret where one of my uncles was living. I thought he could take care of me, but I had to work very hard. This was the time when the pipeline came to Eldoret, bringing oil. My uncle had many problems. I was employed by one of the security companies called Kamalila, which means in Swahili, "to finish." It was 1993 and we were being paid 500 shillings a month (a hard worker today would earn that in a day).

It was about this time I was first arrested. We were taking care of the depot. I was a tall guy of 23 years. The company did not have enough storage space for all the *jerikans* of oil so they piled them outside. One night a thief came when we were sleeping. They took about 20 litres of oil. When we woke up we found that the wire fence had been cut. That morning when we were handing over we did not tell our employer something had happened. After we went home the owners found missing containers. They called the office who came to get us. We were detained by the police and a case was filed. We were charged with stealing and were not able to defend ourselves. My uncle came and released me with a bond. Finally, I won the case.

I went back and stayed one month at my old job. At that time (1994) this company was located behind Raiply, on the western side of Eldoret. I was posted there as a supervisor. Mny companies were coming to build, especially construction companies, and they brought many machines. I was learning to steal. Sometimes people came late at night around 9 pm or very early in the morning to buy things. Instead of protecting the company's property we were selling things, including batteries. Now my colleagues started teaching me how to drink and smoke. Once we were selling *bangi* – opium. The supervisors began discovering many things had been stolen.

While I still worked at the Pipeline, there was a church that guards were protecting. One night, around eleven pm, it was announced that robbers had attacked that mission, so they were asking me to go there to see what had happened. The police were already there. When the office called me, I had to take a guard whom I was supervising. Reaching the gate, I found it open and no one was there, not even the dogs who were usually guarding the place. It was in with confidence. But the thieves were still there, because they had dressed in policeman's uniforms.

The gate was open. I was at the front because I was the commander. On the opposite side of the field where the church stood were homes of the priests and nuns. When I reached the field, I saw somebody I thought was a policeman. As I went towards him, other guards were following me. Suddenly, I realized it was not a policeman; it was a robber. He blocked me with his gun and started shooting. I remember trying to run away, but there was a *kayaba* – prickly fence. I just squatted down and hid. They were looking for someone who had a radio playing. It was mine, but I quickly switched it off.

Now the compound was quiet. Shortly, I saw two people coming. They were talking softly, like they were pushing and harassing somebody. When they passed me, I saw a Catholic sister. One was raping her and the other was standing guard. Unfortunately he saw me. He told me to surrender. He told me, "Go this way." I thought everyone had gone. I thought maybe all of my colleagues were dead, but he was taking me to the place where my friends had been laid. They forced me to walk on there a pile of people. Whoever was caught had been taken there. My friends recognized me. They had been cut badly and the house was full of blood. We waited until around 1 a.m. when I heard a car and someone talking. I realized it was our manager, so I called out and they rescued us.

By 1996 I was an experienced thief. One night we were opposite the police station, behind White Castle, walking towards the estate. Three of us met someone who was walking, carrying a big bag. We didn't care that the police station was near; we robbed that man. Although I had done many robberies this was my first arrest. Sometimes, we had said, "We should have been arrested for much worse things, but this one was a simple one and we were arrested!" I was taken to the police station and charged with robbery. The man we had robbed was an advocate which made it serious. This case was called Robbery/2. If you were found guilty you would be hanged. This man wanted that for us. Though the case was brought in July, there was a long delay. The judge had died while we were waiting for our case to be decided. We had to wait for a new judge to be transferred here from Kitale. By the time he arrived, I had been in custody for one year.

Seven of us were in one ward. When I went to prison, there were only 34 inmates; by the time I came out there were over 300. Robbery had greatly increased. Even preachers were in custody with us. There was an old *mzee,* preacher accused of murder who occupied the next bed. I became like a son to him. One day I told him, "I want to quit smoking." Smoking was not allowed in the prison, but when robbers went to court, there was a way to carry cigarettes.

They asked their families to buy the "roasters." One person could carry 12 packets. They folded the packs and tied them tightly so they could push them through the anus. When a man goes to the prison, they take off all your clothes and inspect you. They cannot detect anything on a carrier, but when the inmate reaches the toilet, he can remove the packs. When that cigarette reaches the prison, one stick is very expensive. The old man told me that he was going to pray for me that I give up cigarettes, so he prayed for me but I could not leave the smoke. He continued to preach. We were not yet in prison, because our cases had not been settled, but we were in what was called "capital remand."

Sometimes, prisoners who had already been in jail came to preach on Saturdays and Sundays. A Luo from the other side came to preach. He preached from the book of Revelation 22:15 which says that outside there are dogs, those who practice witchcraft and others." I couldn't understand what was meant about 'outside.' For us, in prison, we knew being in prison was 'inside' and 'outside' the prison was where we were taken from to be brought inside the prison. I tried to listen carefully so that I could understand why he was saying 'outside' – until he said 'outside Jesus Christ.' He said those who were adulterers, practitioners of witchcraft were outside there.

I could not wait for him to call people who were to be saved. I went to him, weeping, and told him the same words I had told the old mzee who slept beside me on the ward. "I want to quit smoking cigarettes." This prisoner/preacher told me, "I don't want to pray for you that you leave cigarette smoking. I want to pray that you receive Jesus because when you receive Jesus; it means that you have left all your sins." He told me that the cigarette was just a small part – a minor thing. It would be better that I pray to leave sin. I accepted and he prayed for me. When he finished praying for me, I had truly received Jesus, but my colleagues mocked me. Many times when robbers are caught they pretend to be saved, because if you are saved prison warders trust you. It's like you have some favor. Then after coming out of the prison they would go back to being robbers. My friends said it is *wokovu wa jela* (the salvation of prison). They were mocking me, but inside me I knew I had received Jesus. They started counting the days. They said, "Maybe one week." Some gave me two weeks, even one month

Before being arrested I had never read the Bible, but the old man beside whom I was sleeping helped me. He encouraged me to read the Bible, so each time we were in the cell, I read the Bible. God gave me a gift while I was in prison. I started singing. I was the best singer in prison. I would sing while reading the Bible. Brothers came who had already been jailed. Some of them gave me books. I remember one friend, named Boaz Rugut, a Seventh Day Adventist, a Kalengin from Dalat. He brought many books from the SDA. So I read the books and learned some teachings. This lifted my faith. I continued, maybe six months, singing in the choir, in fact leading the choir. Now I had read the Bible and understood some scriptures. When we were locked in the remand, they opened the doors so we could be in the sun as we were rationed sun light.

I started preaching after six or seven months. One day I woke up early in the morning. I preached until my voice went and I could not speak again. I stayed like that for three days until I could speak again. My voice was very low. When I started speaking again, I preached. I prayed asking God to explain what was happening. At that time, I could not understand when God speaks and when he does not speak.

In prison I had friends who had been stealing with me and some others from Uganda who had been there for 10 years waiting for the hearing of their cases. Some are still waiting. Others started planning how they could escape from the prison. I began to listen to them. Actually, I think it was the devil who started speaking to me and reminding me of the past. It had been 1 ½ years. He reminded me how strong I was the other time. I knew how to use guns. So I found myself joining them in planning how to escape from the prison.

Now, I was preaching and they knew I was saved and some of my friends now were saved. My life was now good and smooth, and I was allowed to be free, not locked with the other prisoners. This time was the first time I experienced "back-sliding." We planned our escape for one year. We were all waiting to go to court, but everyone had different dates. We were waiting until we would all go to court on the same date. When that happened we would escape on the way back. It was in August, 1998 we all went to court. This was the day that we vowed we would not go back to prison. We would escape. In the court there are cells for people coming from the police station, people who had ordinary cases, those who had murder cases, and cells for women.

We who were robbers were put in one cell. We planned our escape but knew that to escape from the court would be difficult. We knew where the armor had been put, next to the toile. We decided that one of us would pretend he was going to the toilet. When he reached the place of the armor, we would all come to join him and hold the police. But it could not happen that way.

It was around 4 p.m. and we were now being prepared to be taken back to prison. The distance from the court to prison was about one kilometer. It was on the Eldoret-Iten road. The court is on one side and the prison on the other side. So while we were being arranged to go back to prison, we again organized ourselves so that we were sitting around the corners of the lorry. Each corner had a policeman. We chose strong men to sit next to the police. We were sitting one inside the legs of the one behind us, like dominoes.

We decided that when we reached the main road, and the lorry stopped to let the other cars pass, one person would run out of the lorry. The police would focus on the one person who was running away. Some of us who were sitting in the front of the lorry (we had only one gun) would jump down, waiting for the man with the gun. When he tried to come out we would hold him and run. One of us took the gun, shot, police ran away and we scattered. The four of us did not go very far but waited for another car – a car that was just passing. When they tried to stop that car, the driver refused. They shot at it, but finally stopped another car and hi-jacked it.

While they were going, the driver told them that the diesel was finishing in the car. The one who had a gun saw another car coming behind them. He told the driver not to let that car pass. So, they stopped that car, entered it and went on. Then that driver told them that the petrol was finished. Fortunately there was a petrol station. They went to the petrol station. The attendant came to them. They told him to put in the petrol. When completed, he was returning the key and asking for money, the driver told him to go to the other side to ask the person who had a gun. This man told him, "You bring money." Seeing the gun, he ran away.

They drove until a place called Tarbo Forest. They made sure the driver of that car entered the forest. They left that man there and started walking by foot now till they came up to Webuye. It was daylight. Some had stayed in prison many years so they didn't have much strength. They entered into the sugar plantation. Because they were tired, they slept there. Soon a man came by. He saw people sleeping among the plants. Near that sugar plantation they had a police roadblock and we ran to escape. All of Kenya was alarmed, everywhere, especially in the news media, that Eldoret prisoners had escaped. Many went to the police to report to that they had seen people sleeping in the sugar plantation. It was on the 31st of August when the police came and caught them. They found that the people sleeping in the plantation were among those who had escaped from the prison. I was not among them.

Now, others and myself had taken another route up the hill of the forest and we walked through the crowd. After climbing the hills we came to a flat area so the police went in front of us (because all the town police had been alerted and some were shown the direction we had gone). We did not at first realize that they were policemen because they were far away. They saw our movement from very far because that flatland was a wheat plantation.

We approached a road where we could cross to the other side. There was a man riding a bicycle. I think God used him to save us. There was a car full of policemen. So we changed our direction. The car came fast. When it reached us, the police came out. They were shooting us. Many of the prisoners died. But I was spared. I think

God wanted me to live. I saw many others die.

It had not rained and it was plowing time in the fields. When the whole field was dry because of the sun. When heavy rains come and hit the dirt, then dust comes up like smoke. It was that way when they were shooting at us. I could see something hit before me and the dust came up. After the dust came up, I realized I had heard the sound of a bullet. I remember going down to the hill, coming to another estate called Kamkunji which had an industry called a steel mill. While we were going down, the bullets hit the fence until it went down. When they were aiming at us, the police were shooting, aiming at us but the bullets hit the fence until it went down. Thank God. We were not dead. When we reached the bottom, police were on the other side. I went down pretending I was shot. They carried me and threw me and others who had minor injuries into a car. While I was in the car, we were being beaten with a gun. They were aiming to hit the ribs and wanted to kill us silently. They couldn't kill us directly because there were many people around. I had a wound on my arm and blood started flowing so they thought I was finished.

The next day we were taken to the court again. Those who ran away did some robbery while they were escaping so we were charged with 12 accounts of robbery. Two of them had a gun stolen from the police. The other account was for escaping. We were taken to the judge. They read the charges and we were taken in custody back to the remand.

These were terrible times now because we were kept in tight security. We had brought trouble to the prison. They gave us prison uniforms. On the front and back they wrote "Special Watch" with red letters "S W" so we could be seen from very far. We were set apart. Life became very difficult for us. One day could be like 10 years. At this time, Rev. Simon Koech from the Full Gospel Pentecostal Churches was transferred here from Nakuru. I remember he was teaching about the Holy Spirit, and the need to receive the Holy Spirit. I came to Christ again and was filled with the Holy Spirit.

It was a difficult time because people mocked me. The favor I had before the escape was no longer there. It took many months for them to listen to me. They had seen me first as a preacher. Then I had fallen and tried to escape. Now I was caught again. It was difficult for them to hear me. But some of the brothers who were saved encouraged me, and especially with the help of Rev. Koech, I stood once again. Although we were locked in all day we could still preach inside the wards.

We stayed like this for six months. Then God opened the way for us to be let out for one hour and then we were locked up again. Now that I had been filled by the Holy Spirit, the problem I had had in preaching because of my voice going, was solved. This time, I could preach. The voice could not go. If someone was sick I could pray for them and they were healed. But now it was me who became sick. I became like someone who was going to die. But then the next day I would be ok. Sometimes they gave me some drugs. When I prayed for someone that was sick, the same thing returned to me. So, we went on – I continued to preach and many people got saved. I preached to my friend, who is now a pastor, and he got saved. Now, we faced going to court for the hearing of those 12 accounts of robbery. It took about one year for the case to come to court.

We had a challenge. We came together as brothers, to pray since no one wanted to hear our case. The one who was accusing us now was the government, because the guns that were used were stolen from the police. Many in the prison knew that we could not escape--that we would all be hanged. They told me, "Now, my friend, you will not escape. This time you will be hanged." So, in all of these mockings, I just went before the Lord. I had done wrong. I was saved and I had escaped. I prayed, "If you give me another chance I will do better and I will not go back to prison. But if you let me hang, I will thank you, because I will be with you." Those were terrible days.

Another judge was brought from Kitale. She did not want to see us. We stayed in the prison. We went before her again, and stayed another two months because no one would hear our case. We spent much time in prayer and fasting in prison. We were 32 men. The judges were not agreeing how the case should be tried. It appeared that we were going to be hanged. Whatever happened, I knew I was on the safe side. It seems God was on our side, because many of us were set free, but four people were hanged. Of the original 40 three had already died because of the situation in the prison. At least eight were dead, including some who died when we were captured. The four who were hanged were chosen because when the case was going on, the witnesses had seen them. They were the ones who did robbery while running. Those of us who ran were identified but there were no witnesses against us. That's why we were let free. It was August, 1999, when I was released.

While I was in prison, I preached at night. There was a guard who would listen outside. This guard was pastoring a church in his compound. Each Sunday he would preach the sermon he had heard from us in his own church. Before I was released, he told me that after I was released he would like to work with me. After I was released, we met sometime later. There was a church I knew in Eldoret. The pastor was a friend of the brother of my father.

There was a church I knew in Eldoret. The pastor was a friend of a brother of my father. Although my father's younger brother was not saved, he knew this pastor. When I came out, I remembered that pastor and where he stayed. I went there, because I didn't know anyone else in the town. He and his wife welcomed me and prepared a place for me to sleep because it was late hours. I told them I would not sleep in their house, if I could just stay in the church. So they opened the church and I spent time there praying. In the morning they prepared breakfast and they took me where my father's younger brother (we called him small father) was staying. Unfortunately he was not around. He had gone to Nairobi so I waited for him because I had no money, and needed him to help me with money in order to join my family members. He told his wife to give me transport to go home. I didn't know where I was going. When my parents migrated from Mt. Elgon, after my father's retirement, my father bought an acre of land somewhere. I was directed to the place near the river in Kimileli. They told me the home was across the river, surrounded by banana plantations. As I was approaching the home, I saw an old man and lady sitting in front. I knew they were my parents. They did not recognize me because I had been gone for four years. They thought I was a stranger passing, making a shortcut through the home.

Finally, my mom recognized me. My father thought I was a ghost because one time they had gotten a message that I had died. Because they thought I was dead and buried, they forgot about me. When Mom said, "This is Titus." Father could not believe it. When he finally came to his senses and believed it was really me, they were very happy. Immediately, they called relatives. Now they wanted to make some rituals for me because they believed that I had been with murderers in prison. When my relatives came, my aunts also came. I can still remember what my aunt said, "You were like dead – and when you were in prison you slept together with people who were murderers, killers. Now we need to do some rituals so that you can be cleansed." My parents were brought up Catholic so as I just kept quiet, listening. They didn't know that I was saved. After they finished, I told them, "No ritual is going to be done."

They wanted a sheep to be slaughtered. I told them, "It is true that I've slept with murderers, but if the sheep, when slaughtered, is able to cleanse me, in 1996 when I was caught you should have killed the sheep. If it had that power to cleanse maybe it would have defended me so I would not have been taken to prison. And because the sheep was unable to protect me – or you did not slaughter the sheep to protect me so that I not be taken to prison, let it not be slaughtered. I know who has cleansed me and brought me again to you." Then I told them about Jesus who saved me. My father, being a brought up a Catholic, though he was a drunkard said, "Now no sheep is going to be slaughtered. It is God who has saved him. Leave him alone."

Immediately, the people scattered. Each went his own ways. They expected to eat meat. Now everyone was disappointed. They went away complaining. "Even the father has followed what his son has said." I had no house there because it was a new place.

On that portion of land my father had built two rooms. The kitchen was built of grass, so I spent the night there. The next day I went to see where the church was. I went there and I prayed. The pastor did not know me, but he agreed to open the church so that I could pray there. He was from Zaire, so I had to share with him how I got saved. I thank God because he became close to me. This was around September, 1999.

My younger brother, who followed me 7 times (was the 7th born after me) began to attend church with me. I thank God because that very service they had planned to baptize people. I included myself and we were all baptized in the nearby river. When my brother saw me baptized at the river, he, too, decided to be baptized. He asked me to give him my clothes that I had been baptized in. They thought I was being baptized a second time. That was the day that he was saved. In our family then, we were two believers. Each morning we would awaken about 5 a.m. and pray. In the evening we would pray. They knew who we were, that our parents were drunkards. It was said, "Now, what is happening in that house?" Members would come and discuss the situation.

In October, after staying at home for two months, I became very sick because of the environment in the prison. My parents could not take me to the hospital even though I was dying. My small father lived nearby. He was taking care of a rich person's house. He came and took me to his home. When the church members realized that I was sick and no one would take care of me or take me to the hospital, they came and took me to the hospital. I stayed there about one week. Members came to visit me and even paid my bill. Then I was able to go back to my parents' house.

While I was there, my second brother after me was working at Burnt Forest. He wanted me to go there to find work, but I had no money to go there. He was a carpenter. I was unable to find even ten shillings. I told my sister to look for some money. I had become a burden to them at home, so my youngest sister loaned me 200 ksh which I used for to my brother His wife was at home at his land, and he and the children were staying in town so that the children could go to school He needed me to cook and prepare clothing for him and his children. I did this for some time. I asked him to look for a job for me within the town but he could not find a job for me.

Remember the prison warder who used to listen to me at night? We had agreed that when I came out of prison he would ask me to preach together with him. One day as I was going to town to the main market to buy some food, I happened to meet him. He invited me to preach in his church. I helped him almost one year. We worked hard and the church was growing. When the church grew, he saw that I was getting favor with the members to the point they were almost asking me to be their pastor. So he chased me away and told me not to come back. I thank God, because this was the time I started preaching in buses and at the bus stop. Sometimes someone would invite me to preach at his church. Most of the time I preached at the bus stage.

Fortunately there was a supermarket opening downtown, and my father knew someone. So they hired me at Ukwala Supermarket. This was in 1999. I worked for one week but lost heart because there was no Sunday off. I had to work throughout the week. I remember asking God, "Is this the work that you have given me?" When I was in prison, I asked that I could be given a job so that I wouldn't steal. I was working. I fasted while working. I told God, "Now why do I do this work? Because I have no time to work for you?" I did not finish working there a full week. God answered my prayer.

There was a school—Uasin Gishu Primary School--that needed someone to be a watchman. So my father came where I was working and told me about it. That was on Friday, around 10 in the morning, but when I went to ask the manager to allow me to go out and come back, he refused. My father tried to go there to ask permission for me to go out, too. Finally, my father said, "Just get out, let's go." We went to the school where the interview was to be. I could see God's work in my life. The interviews had ended around 1 pm. It was now 5 pm, but there were still people who had waited for me. They interviewed me and told me to come back again to see if they would take me on Tuesday. On Tuesday I went to the office of the head master. The head master told me, "You go home. You are already employed."

I started working at the school as a watchman, relieving others. I worked three days a week and thanked the Lord because I had time now to preach two days. I went to Kisumu and Kitale to preach. But my colleagues felt jealous now, because I had many off-days. They suggested, "Let's change him to be groundsman." But again, I thanked God because now I had opportunity to preach to children. Sometimes during parade time they would ask me to come and preach to them. In fact they loved me. For the short time I was there, I changed the environment of the school. There was a place that was *maram* with no grasses. I told the head master, "I need grass planted there." It was a good idea at the wrong time. It was Christmas season – there was no rain. "Just let me use the water tank," I suggested. I started digging the place. I planted the grass and watered it for 2 months. When grass started growing then I fenced the place. After the few months, the whole place was green. I planted flowers. The headmaster said to the committee that I was no longer to work as a groundsman. To me, I saw it like a promotion. They made me an office messenger. They bought me a bicycle. Sometime if I child was sick, I took a child to the hospital or him or her to their parents. I did my work well. There was one of the workers who was a drunkard. We were just conversing about God, and God helped me. That guy accepted Jesus. He was a Kisii by tribe. At that time he was living at Kamkunji. He was staying there and after praying with me, he went to show me where he was living. He introduced me to other Kisii's who were saved. One was working with Eagles' Wings Evangelistic team under Neil Lawrence.

We came to meet this guy who was working with Eagle's Wings. He introduced me to Pastor Jairus. I told him all my testimony j and he allowed me to work with him. He had come from Molo and joined Neil. At that time, he had no church. He was a member of Lighthouse church. I joined him. At that time, we started to plan how we could plant a church at Kamkunji. We started to plan how we could plant a church at Kamkunji. We found one house, but the owner had some debts so he was arrested and we couldn't stay. We started a fellowship amd we contributed to buy benches. At that time James Kagari left Lighthouse church to go to Tanzania so Pastor Jairus took over. This was the time that we started to work together. I was one of the leaders. Where the church was, someone gave land so God helped us to get our plot. We had only domestic workers in the group.

I began to be mentored by pastor Jairus. I did not even know how to speak English. Thank God I could lead without knowing English – just speaking Swahili. Sometimes the pastor would go away with Eagles' Wings so I was there to help. He would invite another preacher. And we had people who could interpret. One time the interpreters didn't come to church and pastor had invited a visitor. This was the first time I interpreted in the church. I don't know how it went, but I was able to interpret the preaching. From then on, I started to speak English slowly. A pastor took me to one of the colleges here in town. During the first week, I was almost ready to leave, but one of the students, Adda Wamakal encouraged me. This was also about the time that I met the woman who would be my wife.

How did I get my wife? I was still working as a watchman. When I was around the gate watching, she came, asking for a job. At that time UG primary wanted to start a pre-school. I happened to know that because they were making preparations. When she came to ask me, I gave her a hint that they needed someone because they wanted to start a primary school. I told her the dates of the interviews. There were two ladies who were interviewed. The first lady became head teacher and she became the assistant. They began working together. By that time we knew each other and soon people realized I had married a teacher but I was a watchman. . They made it hard time for us. It separated her from the other teachers. Sometimes she would not come out of the classroom because of what people were saying. Only recently she told me she planned to divorce me. Thank God she did not make that decision. She encouraged herself and stayed.

In 2002 I had been released from the primary school, so I had no work. I kept going to Kapsoya, but in August 2007, I felt compelled to leave. It was very painful because Alex, who was one of the leaders was the first to go. James had also gone out. I was still there because Jairus did not want to let me go.

From Kamkunji we went to Kapsoya. When we got married, my wife came to do the ministry of children at Kapsoya. While in Kamkunji, the landlord wanted to chase us from the house because we had not paid that month's rent. My brother called me to say that he had been caught by the police. He had sent one of my brothers to ask for help to be released. All I had was the 1500 ksh money for the rent. I gave it. The landlord wanted to chase us. I decided we would go to stay in a little room for 500 ksh. When we had saved 10,000 ksh, we looked for land to buy. We got someone who had a car and needed to repair it. He wanted to sell a portion of land, so we agreed and gave him 10,000. We remained with a balance of 13,000. At the end of 2003, we had our own piece of land where we are staying now.

After paying the balance, we started saving money to buy iron sheets. A friend of my father had a house and one of the ladies had a plot in Milene and her husband had died. Because of traditional beliefs, the lady feared to live in that house, so she told my father to find someone to stay in there. I refused to stay in that house because it was 4 miles to town and a long way from Kapsoya. My wife asked me to go there because it was free, but one morning I made the decision.

We went to stay there near Baharini and started building our house on the plot in Milene. My wife was released from work and we had no jobs. Life was difficult.

Not only did my wife have no job, she was also pregnant. I remember using plastic and polyethylene to burn for cooking. She would send children to go around the field where the cows graze and we could pick the dried cow dung plus the plastic bags. That life lasted for two years. I was still at the Kapsoya church, but because we did not have any money for transport, my wife stayed at home. Myself, I thank God for that time. I would wake up each morning at 6 am wondering where I could go. We had no food.

We did not take any breakfast but would go to Kapsoya, visit people, and witness to them. In the evening at 7 pm I could come back home, but when pastor used to give me money for transport, and I knew we had nothing at home, I could not take the vehicle, I would walk instead of using the money. When I got to town, I would buy maybe some sugar and then walk home. Sometimes when he went out, Pastor Jairus left me in charge. In August 2007, Pastor Jairus when he was going to Mombasa for a crusade he left me in charge. I remember when he was going to a meeting, I told him I had something I wanted to share with him. We sat at the side of the road. I told him that I felt like now I should go to Baharini to plant a church. He did not answer me.

After keeping quiet for a long time, he asked me why. I thanked him for the time I'd had with him, for the many ways he had helped me. During the two years, I had been at Kapsoya, my family was going elsewhere to church. I felt it was not good, that I needed to be with my wife in the same church. He said he was willing to commit himself to pay for the transport for both me and my wife. I thought, "Now he has got me." But I had another reason. I told him about my family; both of us had no jobs.

He told me again that he was willing to provide everything that I needed. I said, "I need to go. It is my time." There was a plan for building a church, and when the time would come, we would have the plot. He said that he was not going to answer me that time. He came back after two weeks, and I waited for another week, thinking that maybe he would answer me. He kept quiet. Finally, we sat where we

Tea Without Sugar: Chastened for a Destiny

had sat the other time. He told me that now because I had that fire going, he had nothing to hold me. "When do you feel that you should plant that church?" I told him, the coming two weeks, on the 27th of August.

Pastor Jairus summoned the district pastors. He told them about the plan for me to start a church. That Sunday before we dismissed, they prayed for my wife and I. Jairus asked if I had a house. I told him I'd found one. He gave me 3,000 ksh. Pastors and some of my friends from Kapsoya came and the church was launched. We were almost thirty the first day. In that village, all of us were foreigners. We had no money. My wife said, "What can we do about eating?" "God will provide. You go to the nearby shop. Tell the owner to give us two crates of soda and some bread. We will pray." My wife went and got them. People ate and drank and were satisfied. When they gave the offering, we paid the offering and there was not any left. But we still were in faith.

At that time, God spoke to me to start preaching in the morning, because Pastor had assisted me with a small amplifier and one of the brothers, Tom Myaka, of the Eagles' Wings Team, had a speaker that he gave to me. My house was on the top of the hill, I put my speaker on the top of the roof. I was in the house but people could hear me all around. The second Sunday came. I went early in the morning, set up the equipment I had, put on the tape to play songs that could be heard from afar. I remember I was sitting praying, but I was looking out to see if someone was coming. My wife prepared a nearby room to make it a Sunday School room. The place was like a computer college which someone had started. After that, I told her to go to the other room. My children were there. I saw one woman. I thanked God because he had brought her. We went on praying, and interceding. Another woman coming and thanked God. We continued to pray and another woman came.

When they reached three, we stopped praying and started the Bible study. As we continued, another woman came. By the time we finished there were eight women. Then my wife and children came. We sang and I preached again. By the end of the service, we were twelve people.

We kept on. I started doing house to house evangelism and

preaching every day with an amplifier from my house. If I traveled, my wife preached in the morning. I realized that many were getting the message in the morning. Some couldn't imagine who this man was who was preaching from the hill. I believe this is one thing God used to help the church to grow. In October, Pastor Enoch Barudi invited me to speak at his church's lunch hour meetings. At that time my finances were not strong. On Wednesday I reached a place called Milene – about 4 to 5 km. from Baharini. I was just singing a song, "Mungu wangu wewe wa jua kwa nini nyapitia haya." (My God, you know why I am passing through all this.)

I reached town near the hall and rested, leaning on the wall. One man came and I shared with him. He was also attending that lunch hour meeting. Afterward a person came and opened the door, so we started praying. After sharing my testimony, God touched him. He immediately asked me, "Are you willing to allow me to buy you a bicycle?" I thanked him, and we went to the supermarket where he bought me a new bicycle. The next day he came to my house. Before we departed, he said, "Tomorrow we shall meet."

I had already talked to the landlord. Our place was small. He had a big plot and a field there. I asked him if we could build a temporary structure. I took the money from the brother, went to the timber yard and came to Discipleship College to meet Pastor Jairus. Then we borrowed a tent from Gordon Bloodworth. He gave us four tents so we constructed a temporary building. By that time we had 40 members. The tent structure was full within two months. After building the tent, we went on with fellowship. It was November and because three of the tents were sacks, they were rotten from exposure to the rain and sun. We could be seen from the outside while we were in the service. I was praying, "God what can we do?"

At that time, people were preparing for the elections of 2007 to choose a president and MPs. It was campaigning time. In December, after the election, fighting began. Most of the people in our church were from different groups and they all left. I remained alone with my wife. My children were then at my wife's home for the holidays. That day I was at home because there was no where you could go. We had no food. One woman from the indigenous people heard from the group who were causing trouble that they were planning to come and chase me.

The reason is that I used to make noise in the morning. I asked her, "Is that the only reason why they want to burn my house?" At first my wife was crying. I told her, "If that is the only reason why they want to burn my house I will not go." She also told that woman, "We won't go if that is the reason. Let them come. There is nothing in my house I am going to transfer anywhere." I waited. No one came. I didn't see anyone. We stayed. No food. Even if we had had a family, there was no way to bring food to us. I'd call Pastor Jairus, but he'd say, "How can I bring food to you?" There were many refugees that time. In that situation, I relied on God. One evening Brother Gordon called, asking, "Where are you? " Gordon managed to bring food to my house. It was enough for a month. Aaron, a missionary brother at Discipleship College and his wife also came with a car to my house to bring food for us. We were still renting the church. Aaron gave me 6,000 ksh and paid for six months of church rent. I did not have to think about the church or the church rent. The situation went on. We had some people who ran from other places and came to our church. Afterwards some of them were hiding in the bushes. Some were neighbors. God enabled us to hide them in our house for awhile. Others, we took to the neighbors.

When Gordon heard about that, he went to Kapsoya for food. We knew the houses where people were hiding. We could give them, as well as others, clothes and food. We were helping people. Anything I could get from friends, I divided with some of the people that were affected by the clashes. When the clashes ended, we began starting another church. All the members of the first church had left. We went house to house to evangelize. Their hearts were still hurting – they had pain in their hearts. One Sunday in the midst of the service, around five women came and joined our fellowship. When the service ended, they told me told me they came from a nearby church after they discovered it was closed. Their pastor had gone because of the clashes. The next week, they declared they would continue with us, so we received them as members and they are with us until today.

God helped us as time went on to have a small plot. We transferred from the tent to the plot which I got when I was ministering at the lunch hour meetings to town. There was a brother named Branton who was fellowshipping there. We preached together in Christ the Rebuilder Church. He and his father gave the money for us to build on that plot. It was a portion of an acre, not square, but more like a road. The owner wanted to sell three of these plots of land, but because we did not have the money to buy all, we agreed that I would pay by installment to buy the whole piece of land.

A businessman approached him to buy the land for a business. I was shocked to receive that message. It was 2008. I had invited a teacher of Discipleship College and she brought another missionary. The church was praying about the situation. I told her that we had until Monday morning to come up with the money. On Tuesday morning I was in the church praying. Around one o'clock, I received a phone call from another of the missionaries. She was not in the church, but she got the report from the missionary fellowship, that they were praying for that issue. I told her what had happened so she told me to wait for a moment. She called me again and told me to meet them at Baker's Yard.

She told me I would meet someone who was tall, another missionary. I met them and we talked. They agreed to pay for the plot. While we were talking, they asked me to call the owner. At that exact time, the owner of the plot was bargaining with that businessman.

I was ready to pay. A witness for the businessman was a lady from my church. When I was calling the owner of the plot, he was telling me to wait and the lady was asking him who was calling. He did not know that that lady belonged to my church. He told her the person was the owner of the tent church. She told him, "If you had agreed you would sell it to the church, don't sell it to the businessman." When that lady told him that he shouldn't change his word to the church, the man stopped and called me. He asked me where I was. He came. I had almost half the funds and gave him the money. After three days, we completed the transaction. From that time, it was like God opened the way.

One evening, I received a call around seven from the man who had given me the money and asked me whether I had a desire to go to school. I told him, "I desire it, but financially, I can't." He told me to come to school and register. My wife had 2,000 shillings. She told me,

"You will need to take some money." She had 2,000 shillings. "You will need to take some money. Pay what you have. When you come back we'll look to see where we can find the money." I registered my name. I waited but nobody asked me for money

I came the next day to begin school. I didn't know who was paying my school fees. I stayed there almost six months without knowing who was paying my schooling. When I went to the cafeteria they told me, "Your lunch is paid." Up to now, the cafeteria has not told me who paid the bill. They were given money for a certain period then stopped paying for me after that time. I received a call asking if my wife desired to go to ECDE, because the school was planning to start ECDE. My wife was willing to go and finished the Care Giver's Course. I thank God, because another miracle came. For a long time, she had desired to go on with her desire in children's ministry. She had another chance to go on to a diploma course. Thank God, because both of us were now students at Discipleship College.

While I was in prison, I told God that if he I would be released from prison, and he gave me another chance, I would go back to preach in the prison. Often, when people were released, they commit robbery and go back to prison. I didn't want to come back that way. I wanted to come back to preach as a free man. After planting one church I applied for permission but received no reply. One of my spiritual mentors was the chaplain who helped me get into the prison. It was not easy. He told me to organize with the church members to plan a fund-raiser for buying books, Bibles, soaps, etc. In less than two weeks, we were given permission because we were bringing things. In March of 2010, the church donated those things.

I was now allowed to go into the prison.. They knew that I was a robber, plus I had tried to escape. They were afraid that I had another agenda. I applied for permission to visit both women and men. The women in charge (who is saved) accepted me. While I was there the person in charge of women (who is saved accepted me and while there told me of their need. The office of the assistant in charge did not have a table. I knew that in the men's prison there is a workshop. I gave 5000 ksh to the men's prison work shop. They paid for the men's industry to make a very good table. It has written on it, "Given by New Testament Church of God." The assistant insisted that the table be put in the office of the one who was in charge, who was a Muslim. This was how we got into the women's prison. We bought sandals for the children and Bibles. We finished that mission.

In June I met with my spiritual father at the prison. I asked him, "How can I get in the prisons?" He knew the people in charge and told me to apply again. I organized with the church and we applied. That time they accepted to go to the men's prison where there are about 1,000 inmates. We preached there and many were saved. Thank God we had Bibles, soap, and toilet paper to give them. I spoke boldly, "What do you think, if we bring a Bible School here?". The one in charge of the prison didn't want a Bible School, but told us to apply. We were allowed to come but with some conditions. So today, the CIMS (Certificate in Ministerial Studies) courses are being taught and we have an official permit from the commissioner of the prisons in Kenya.

God has helped bring the Gospel through a small vessel like me. Now, the guards are getting taught the CIMS classes. After many of the 15 guards are being taught the CIMS class, they are being transferred. When they are being transferred, they can teach the prisoners in their assignment. God is using those who are trained to teach others. We are being multiplied. They won't need permission to go because they are already working as guards.

I have the idea to plant another church where my wife came from. We have surveyed it and one of my church members has decided to pay for a room for four months. We will begin with a crusade. We know God will make a way, as He has always done before.*

*At this writing not only has this second church been planted but at least one more. The second was launched on the slopes of Mt. Elgon on December 12, 2011. To God be the glory!

Tea Without Sugar: Chastened for a Destiny

A PIECE OF CHARCOAL
John Kagwe

The problem with stories is that they can become very long and I think my story is one of those, so I hope you will bear with me. I was born in 1978 on Lamu Island. When I was 2 years old we moved to Nabkoi. It was during that time (1985 and 1986) that I started to go to Sunday School where we were taught about God. My parents were members of the Full Gospel Churches of Kenya where my father served as a church elder. Practically speaking, that was like being a pastor, because one pastor oversaw a large area and relied on elders to help him shepherd the flock. My "first" conversion was in 1986 when I heard my father preach in an open air meeting. My mother had told me not to go because she thought that the issues were those of adults and not of children. She thought I wouldn't understand the message of salvation. Later, this became a discouragement to me to the point that I began to think that I had not been born again properly since my mother thought I had not been of age.

In 1988 we left Nabkoi for Eldoret town and I continued attending Sunday School for children at a church member's house because the church itself was far from our place. When Reinhardt Bonnke came to Eldoret in 1992 I heard the message of the gospel and I decided to dedicate my life to Christ once more. It was after that meeting that I felt my heart filled with joy – so much joy that I smiled on my own as we walked all the way home that day.

But the Lord had more for me. In 1993 we went to a church convention called "Church Ablaze" in Nakuru and it was in this meeting hosted by a preacher called Reverend Irungu that I was filled with the Holy Spirit. We had always been prayed for in the Full Gospel Church to receive the Holy Spirit. Sometimes we would be told to kneel down, sometimes to stand up with our hands raised and I wondered which the right way was. I was very amazed to see people praying earnestly and speaking in other tongues. I had been told that if you did not speak in other tongues you had not received the Holy Spirit and I really wanted to receive the Spirit. I had been prayed for by evangelists so many times that I had become discouraged and thought that God did not love me enough to give me the Holy Spirit. It was at the convention in Nakuru on the third day that there was an altar call for those who wanted to be filed with the Holy Spirit. I walked over to the front where there was a prayer line. Again, I was told to kneel down. A group of preachers walked from the left to the right praying for people. The instructions given by the preacher were not to pray for anything except to give thanks for the gift of the Holy Spirit. When they prayed for the woman who knelt beside me, she began to talk in other tongues and was filled with the Holy Spirit. When they prayed for me I did not feel anything extraordinary and so they passed on to the woman on my right side. When they prayed for her, she also began to talk in other tongues also. Once more I told God, "You do not love me. You have denied me the gift of the Holy Spirit once more." As I walked to the 8th row where I had been sitting suddenly it was like someone poured cold water on my head. It seemed like it was flowing all over my body. I started shaking and I felt my face crinkle up. When I tried to open my eyes they were filled with tears and I burst forth speaking in other tongues. That night I did not want to sleep. I wanted to continue speaking in my new language. I spent four hours praying.

In 1994 I joined form I at Uashin Gishu high school. That year I evangelized 12 of my classmates who received Christ. In form II I became the organizing secretary for Christian Union in the school. In form III I continued holding that post and also trained the choir. In form IV I became the chairman of the Christian Union.

All through my secondary school it was difficult for my parents who had seven other children to provide us with lunch, so many times we skipped the meal. Most of those lunch times found me sitting under a tree reading the Bible. Whenever I got money for lunch it was not enough for a decent meal so I ate day-old bread with water because it was cheaper. Being the CU chairman was a great experience for me in that I saw the conversion of even Moslem students in the school. When I left secondary school in 1997 I was worried that I would not be having anything to do in the meantime and as the saying goes, "An empty mind is the Devil's workshop." So I started praying and fasting alone in the woods, seeking wisdom for my future. At this time we lived in a place called Kapsoya. After a two-day fast I was invited to share the Word of God in a home fellowship. Only three women came to the home fellowship but I was happy to share from the book of Acts, chapter 2. After I shared for approximately 40 minutes we stood up and prayed and two of the women were filled with the Holy Spirit and began to speak in tongues. One of the women – the cell group leader – began screaming. I was worried about the screaming so I tried to drown the noise by singing a chorus. It was to no avail. Boys that were playing football came running and surrounded the house. When they heard me sing they also joined in singing. This experience left me wondering if this was the line that God wanted me to take – to become a pastor.

Next I became a member of a Pentecostal Church called Church on the Rock. There I served as a member of the praise and worship team. After a year, in 1999, I was chosen to be the youth chairman. This church was located in town center and it was comprised of people who came from a higher standard of living than mine. Because of this, I was afraid to lead them, so I rejected the offer at first. But the next Sunday the pastor called me to come forward and prayed for me in front of the congregation. He cited that no one in the Bible considered themselves to be worthy of being a leader – not Jeremiah or even Moses. But because of the fear I had of leading this group of youth, I retreated into prayer and fasting so that God would give me strength to lead them. I began to see God move in our youth meetings in a powerful way. Children were healed. Older people were healed from sicknesses. And the youth team grew from 24 members to 96 members in just 2 years.

But winds of change were blowing. In 2002 I left that church due to a crucial change in doctrine. The pastor had gone to a conference in Nairobi and met with some ministers from South Africa who introduced to our church the apostolic reformation. When the pastor's wife stood to introduce the pastor, she said that in the desert when the Children of Israel complained to the Lord; the Lord sent snakes and many were bitten, but God told Moses to make a bronze snake and whoever looked at the bronze snake would be healed. One day the cloud began to move and they were supposed to follow the cloud. As they moved a number were left behind looking at the bronze snake but did not follow the cloud so they were not in God's will. Hence, what was once a blessing had now become idol worship because they did not follow the leading of the Holy Spirit. It was at this juncture that she said God had moved and clearly the statement meant that since God has moved we must also move. From the scriptures I was aware that God is the same yesterday, today and forever, but from her statement seemed to me to be saying God had changed. And she told us that the days of miracles were over because the cloud had moved. She said prayer and intercession were not very important any longer either. The important thing was having the right building. She said Noah was given a blueprint to build the ark and persevered for 120 years building it in the midst of mockery and scorn. But one day the floods came and they were saved. They had built what saved them. Then she added, we are building what is going to save us. Now, all through my life I had been taught that salvation is based on the finished work of the cross but it seemed this was now changing. I had been taught that prayer is very necessary for a Christian's growth that is why I spent a lot of time in prayer and fasting. This new doctrine made me feel like my heart had been pierced with a sword and left to bleed.

In my discouragement, I decided to leave town to take some time off and to see what God wanted. I joined a church in Kinangop and began playing keyboard for them and leading a cell group. At this time I was settled that God was calling me to ministry. So I went to my father and told him I wanted him to pay for my Bible School but he did not feel it was a good idea and tried to discourage me. I had been offered a chance to have a scholarship by the International Pentecostal Holiness church where I had ministered often, but I was afraid of my father.

While I was in Kinangop I had a lot of problems, having no food to eat or clothes to wear. However, the church did pay for my house rent. My mother was worried about me and called me home to take me to college. At this time because of the difficulties I had passed through I decided to comply and leave ministry alone. So I went to Alphax College and did a computer repair and maintenance certificate. My internship was to be in Kabarnet. My father had given me 1000 shillings. I was given a job at which I worked for 6 months with full pay. But then, the burden for ministry was growing in me and I was feeling horrible that I had run away from the calling of God. Eventually, I left Kinango and joined a church in Kapsoya called FPFK that is Free Pentecostal Fellowship in Kenya. While I was in Kabarnet they started a church in nearby Mosoriot. I was called to go there to join full-time ministry as a salaried assistant pastor.

I took a church of about 100 people in Mosoriot. By this time I had met the lady I wanted to marry. So I had two projects in front of me. I wanted to serve as a minister but the people of the region had thought I was not qualified enough because I was not married. They kept pressuring me to marry so that I could attend to their children and wives and also speak to men. I had worked for several months without any pay. The pastor who had sent me there came every Sunday to collect the money after the service. On Sunday afternoons I used to walk to homes of the church members asking for food. They were basically farmers so few members were employed. They didn't have enough money to pay even for my house rent. In the meantime, the overall pastor had a disagreement with the members and they started leaving the church, one by one.

One time I decided to walk to that pastor's home to tell him that disagreements were hurting the church. From that time forward he had a "bone to pick" with me. As the church continued to decrease in number I grew more and more discouraged. One morning members came to me and told me that the whole church community had left, together with their families. I was left with 6 members. I decided to give up on the church and told the pastor to pay me my dues. He told me there was no money. I asked him what had happened that I had not been paid for a period of about eight months? He told me that it was my own fault: I was not able to do the work and that was why the members had left.

Meanwhile, only three weeks were remaining until my wedding ,but marriage plans had also hit the rocks. The lady I was going to marry came from the Kalenjin community. Her name was Caroline Chepchirchir, a great woman of God, an intercessor and a soloist at IPHC. Most of my community did not support my inter-tribal marriage. They thought I was not listening to them. However, my parents, being Christians did not have a problem with it although my mother did seem to worry and asked me to pray. The girl's parents did not support the wedding, either. Her mother said that all the Kalenjin married to Kikuyu men were usually abandoned. And since our communities had not been seeing eye to eye for a long time, they were not in support of it. When I went to pay dowry I was asked for 12 cows instead of the customary 3 or 4. They cited that I was a Kikuyu, therefore rich. Being a pastor with no income had been a great challenge for me. I therefore did not have the cows to pay and so I set up a committee to help me raise money for them. However, the committee for the wedding and the dowry collapsed. Thankfully, we had raised at least enough money for 3 cows by the time it failed. Finally, my parents went to talk with the girl's parents. After a grueling 5 hours, they agreed to give me the girl without my paying the full amount. It was my wife who had discovered that the wedding committee had failed. Undaunted, she set up a committee on her own. That committee of six people raised 42,000 ksh (about $450) which we used for the wedding. By that time, I had left my church, so, with only two weeks left before my wedding, I joined the lady's church. When the time came in August, 2005, I wedded. (Note: Kenyan men wed, women are wedded).

My previous pastor did not show up at my wedding. However the members who had left that church attended the occasion. After my wedding IPHC took me as a youth pastor and paid for my rent. I was, however, to look for funds to pay for my bills and support my family. I did not have a job. My wife's job had also ended just two months before our wedding. As a result, we had problems trying to put food on the table, but we were happy!

I was called back to Mosoriot by the members who had left the church and I found they had started a new church under a tree at a place called Ndurot. They were all from the Nandi community (a branch of the Kalenjin) and even though I came from the Kikuyu community they asked me, after much discussion, to be their pastor. Now, I ran a church under a tree and we had many meetings together. IPHC graciously offered covering for the little church. The offering from this church could only pay for fare back and forth from Eldoret. Even when they took a special offering it would not support me. Unfortunately, they had not learned how to give. We had a fund-raising to build a church because the rains and sunshine were interfering with the services. The owner of the piece of land where we were meeting had given us .2 acre to build the church. However, he was a polygamous man and did not want a Kikuyu pastor. He actually wanted to be the pastor himself, however, the other members of the church thought it was not proper for him to be the pastor as a polygamous man. He therefore stopped supporting the cause of preaching the gospel in the area and left the church. During the day of the fund-raising he showed up and gave me 5 shillings for building the church. However, God helped us. We raised enough money for 27 iron sheets. A member of the church also gave us a tree. Some youths had a power saw and they decided to make timber out of that tree. The only needed items remaining were building nails and labor for building. However, when the owner of the plot saw that we were going to build only a wooden church for the community he gave the land to another church. So we were left meeting under the tree. Meanwhile he also joined the neighboring church. It was at this time I decided to ask him about the plot. His answer was that I was not a member of the community and therefore the church would sit down and discuss the issue because they did not want me there any longer. At this time we had reached around 35 members. I collected my church equipment and left. The church leaders met and talked about it but they couldn't agree. Therefore they stayed in their own homes waiting for a solution. The owner took our 27 iron sheets and gave them to his brother. In that fund raising I'd given more than all of them. Now I was wondering how God would allow me to go on from there. The man who received the iron sheets was a drunkard, to the point that he was not even building his own house even though it was raining. I came back to the area three months later to ask them whether they had reached an agreement whether or not to start a new church, but they were all discouraged and didn't want to start a new church. I encouraged them to attend a church in the area and I would come to escort them. One of the women in our church went to the landowner to ask him why he had taken the iron sheets. In her explanation she told him that God would punish him for what he had done. But the man answered, that if he would be punished by God he would be the one to feel the pain, not her. However, this man is now dead. He fell from the roof of his storage shed and died while trying to chase after a daughter who had acted inappropriately. The Mosoriot members ended up joining the Full Gospel church but I stayed at IPHC, serving the youth.

My wife was expecting our first child and we still had difficulty putting food on the table because the church only paid the house rent. We had tried to sell French fries beside the road but the price of potatoes was so high that we would make very little profit at all - only 20 shillings after 4 hours (less than $1). After 3 weeks of struggle we abandoned the business. I was looking for anyone who would give me employment to supplement my church work, but I couldn't find anyone. Finally, I asked for a job to dig the trenches for a fiber optic cable, but I didn't even have a hoe for digging. For our upkeep I used to walk to town and try to locate friends to ask them for help. At the time it didn't occur to me that I had become a beggar. I would go to a church compound where there was a Bible school and I would up pick charcoal up that had been thrown from the kitchen "store" and we would use that for cooking our food. My mother actually kept us alive with food. One day I walked into the compound of the Bible school and there was no charcoal, so I walked to the tarmac road next to Kenya Creameries Company and as I stood beside the road I saw bicycles carrying charcoal coming down the road. Whenever a bicycle hit the pot-holes on the tarmac road, two or three pieces would fall down. I realized I had seen a miracle! So I walked to the nearby fence and picked up a plastic bag that was caught there and started walking along the road collecting the pieces of charcoal which had fallen off the bicycles. I was crouched down busy picking up the charcoal when I saw the feet of a woman standing in front of me. With pieces of charcoal in my hand and a plastic bag nearly half full I looked up to see it was Mrs. Kurui, a friend of my mother. They had been teaching together in a primary school. She was also a friend to my wife's family, who were considered wealthy. She greeted me, "Praise the Lord, pastor." With embarrassment on my face, I replied, "Amen." When she left, I asked God, "Why are you doing this to me? Is this what you do to people who follow you? " I was very embarrassed. But I went back home with the charcoal. The next time I saw her, I made sure she didn't see me.

I requested my mother to give me money to start a vegetable

vender business. She gave us 500 shillings. With an additional 100 shillings we managed to buy not only vegetables but also made a 350 shillings wooden structure for a shop. This business was very successful. We bought vegetables for 35 shillings and sold some for as much as 250 shillings. Our customers were the students of a nearby university and soon the food problem in our house was eliminated.

However, the neighboring shops were also selling vegetables and because we were competing with them, taking away their customers, they hired a shepherd boy to kick down our vegetable stand. In the morning I would find the stand leaning on its side. I would look for ropes and tie it and make it stand up again. But one day, he jumped on top of it and broke it down completely. I realized if I built another one they would do the same, so I talked to the premises owner to give me a more sturdy shop so that I could also sell general foodstuffs. My mom advanced me 10,000 shillings and this shop became a great success. My son had already been born and my family was growing well.

But at the church I was not contented because of a few things that were happening. It was my opinion that people who were engaging in sinful behavior were not being rebuked, making immorality to thrive in our church. In addition my salary was very little. Fortunately, at this time a church elder had gone to Australia for medical treatment for his son's eyes. When he was in Australia he met people from a church called Southland International Christian Center in Melbourne City. They offered to start a church in Kenya at Eldoret Town Center. The elder came and asked me if I was willing to join him as an assistant pastor to start a new church. I walked to my senior pastor and told him a man that cannot feed his wife is worse than an infidel because when our son was sick we couldn't even afford to take him to the hospital. He agreed. But I knew there would not be a change, so we moved to the town center with Pastor Y and started a church. The first Sunday we had 23 people at Wagon Wheel. However, by the fourth Sunday we were given notice to vacate because our singing and worship were causing the drunkards to keep off from the bar. So we went to Grand Pri Hotel in the same town. We also were given notice to leave within the next two weeks for the same reason. We finally were able to get premises in town in a classroom belonging to Eldoret

Polytechnic for which we paid 2000 shillings per month. Actually we were only paying for electricity. This really seemed like a gift from God.

In the meantime God had provided a job for my wife. She was now working with Associated Motors as a secretary. In doing so she became the sole bread winner of our home. In 2007 my wife went to her village to vote. I was somehow uneasy myself since I stayed in an estate full of members of the Kalenjin community. My tribe, Kikuyu, was associated with the government. So when I saw the noise on the television, that people were protesting the re-election of our Kikuyu president, I locked my house and went to stay with a friend in Pioneer Estate. Immediately, as soon as the president was inaugurated, clashes began. My pastor had told me to go to the airport to fetch some visitors from Australia but I was uneasy about it so I declined. They barely reached town before an electric pole was hauled before them to block their way. They were all told to alight to identify themselves, and to tell which tribes they came from. I believe I was miraculously saved from death. Fortunately the protesters were confused by the names and so the people who went to fetch them escaped, too.

During the 3 weeks of clashes in Kenya I stayed in Pioneer Estate where we slept outside guarding the houses where we had taken refuge. Later I became very sick with malaria because of it. I used to go to see my mom at the refugee camp at the Show Grounds (Fair Grounds) where she took refuge with thousands of others after her area had been burned down. My mom's village is next to Kiamba, the place where a church filled with people who had taken shelter had been burned down with the people in it. Prior to that God had miraculously saved my mother by directing her to a school where she and about 5000 people had taken refuge. Now she was at the Show Grounds. Women who had taken refuge there tried to convince me to leave my wife because she came from the wrong community. They argued that my wife knew but did not tell us that there were going to be clashes since they believed that all Kalenjin knew there would be war. But my wife and I wouldn't just let the voices of people destroy our family. At this time we kept talking to each other on the phone and encouraging each other. Finally, after the war my wife came back home. The church still had those 21 guests from Australia, who were shifting from one location to another because of insecurity. However, food had become very expensive and I didn't get to meet the visitors during this time. We only met on Sunday's. By this time our business had run down due to the tribal animosity which had begun months before the clashes. We were supposed to be salaried pastors together with the senior pastor, but we had gone six months without pay. I had hoped to meet with the visitors from Australia to discuss about church progress and upkeep but this was not possible and therefore they had left before we had talked. I went to my senior pastor's house to ask about the promises they had given us for our upkeep as ministers but he answered that they promised strongly that they would send it for us.

Soon we left the building for which we were paying only 2,000 ksh – for a bigger building for church services. The monthly rent was 65,000 ksh and yet as a family we didn't have any upkeep. So, three months later I transferred with my wife to Pastor Y's church because my house was in arrears. My pastor still promised that the Australian church had committed themselves that they would pay.

In 2010 God blessed us with a second child, called Rachel. At this time I discovered that funds had always been sent to Pastor Y's personal account. It happened that when we had started the church he had given me his email and password to be typing for him because he was not a very good typist. Therefore I went and checked whether there were funds that had come in and I discovered that funds had always been sent, but we were always left out as a family. As the assistant pastor I called for a committee to plan for a church anniversary. While we were discussing the budget, the pastor kept telling us to raise money and therefore I asked him to request the Australian church to give us money. When he kept saying, "They have no money," I decided to tell him the truth, that money had always been sent and he had been lying to the church, the committee and to me. After the meeting Pastor Y took money and dished it out to the committee members and asked me to leave the church. We continued going to church there for several Sundays but he did not address the issue. His son took over as the assistant pastor and I was just a member, but this had happened without any communication. I agreed with the church members that we didn't want any more lies from the pulpit and therefore we decided to not have a sermon from the pulpit for the following Sunday. Since I had the support of about 75% of the members, we planned that one of the church members would tell the pastor to not preach to us but to sit down for a church meeting which we had never had in the church. But when the church elder stood to talk, he said, "I don't know why our church pastor is not seeing eye to eye with Pastor John so we would like to sit down and talk about it." Pastor Y stood from the place where he was sitting and told him he could sit down. The church elder sat down and I realized that I had lost the opportunity to have the whole body sit down and have a business meeting. I shot up from my seat. Pastor Y was already holding the microphone. I also picked up a microphone and told him, "We don't want any more sermons." When I saw him coming towards me to take the microphone I picked up a plastic chair and raised it upwards and moved away from him. I was speaking loudly, "You lied to us that someone gave us these plastic seats as a gift while it was the Australian partners who sent the money. On that day we clapped for you because we had seen a miracle, but the miracle was a lie. We do not want more lies. We want the truth. We will not build on the wrong foundation. We will build on the truth." A pastor friend of his who had visited the church stood up and asked me to sit down because I was standing on the holy place and I could either get a blessing or a curse from that place. After he asked me to sit down he convinced me there would be a meeting in the afternoon.

That afternoon, after Pastor Y had sent the majority of the church members home, he addressed the complaining group and said he didn't know who I was and that I was not a pastor in that church. My response to that was clapping and saying, "You have just spoiled everything." The meeting could not go on, so we left after Pastor Y promised he would see each person individually. He later came to me and said that if I came to his church again he would call the police.

I therefore left the church and stayed home. I was very discouraged. My mom came home to check on her children and learned that I was no longer going to church and so she prayed for us. The words in her prayer came from the story of Isaac where Isaac would dig wells but the enemies would throw stones into them and take them so that Isaac would dig wells and never drink the water. I was too discouraged to even pray for myself and was tired of hopping from church to church.

It was then I got employment as the manager of a guest house. I really did not know the customers who used to go there. When I found the truth, I discovered it was a place which was frequented by prostitutes and so for 6 months I rented rooms to them. It seems they had an arrangement that the prostitute would bring a client who would pay and then I would return the amount that had been paid for the room by the prostitute. My wife was happy that there was now food in the house. I had written a complaint to the church in Australia but Pastor Y had explained that I had become insane. They had also written telling me that we should solve the issues as soon as possible and they would not meddle because he was the "man on the ground." However, after about six months a team of the Australian partners was visiting the city. I had been praying to God for myself to be back in ministry. I happened to meet some of the Australian partners in a supermarket in Eldoret. They asked me what had happened and I explained that Pastor Y was corrupt. However, they did not seem to believe me. I did give them a contact number in case they needed to hear the story.

On Sunday several of the church members who had been expelled from the church asked me to go back to church with them so that we could meet with the Australian team. We didn't have a plan on how to meet them so I chased after the missions coordinator and gave him a piece of paper showing him that there was corruption in the church. That Sunday at 4pm, I was called to Marriot Hotel and it is there I met with the pastor from Australia, the missions' coordinator, Pastor Y, a church elder and my wife. I explained how we had paid 2,000 for the hall where we met but Pastor Y had said that we paid 35,000 so he was told to explain what had happened, but he kept quiet. The missions' coordinator could not control himself; he slipped from his seat, put his face on the floor and began to weep like a baby. He looked at the pastor through tears in his eyes and said, "Do you know what you have done to us?" And then he said, "When we go back to Australia and explain what you have done they are going to say we are idiots." And Pastor Y answered, "No they won't." Afterwards, the coordinator said, "This story was ridiculous." He said, "This must be a lie." Pastor Y said, "Yes, Pastor John is lying. " Pastor Y was then told to produce documents on what he had done with the money for the last 2 years. He did not have any documents to show, while I produced receipts to show all the payments I had made until that time. The visitors from Australia were crushed. They decided to go and sleep. They promised to leave this corrupt country immediately. But the following day in the evening they called me to ask me whether I wanted to go back to preaching the gospel. My answer was affirmative and so they asked me to close down that church – Eldoret International Christian Centre - and to start a new church. That is how Abundant Grace Fellowship, the church where I'm now ministering, started.

Our partners gave me ksh 18,000 to go and register the church. The country was embroiled in corruption and pastors were paying up to ksh 150,000 for the same document. However, I went to the Attorney General's office, paid ksh 2,000 shillings and then I had my uncle who worked for the government call them to ask them to help me. After 6 months I was presented with a church registration certificate. This was a great miracle. The remainder of the money was used for transportation, preparing the constitution and other expenses incurred in getting the registration.

The church was having approximately 30 members but then we had some of the members who were supporters of the former pastor who conspired with him to oust me. They wrote to the missions' coordinator telling him that I was more corrupt than the pastor. They said all the money they had been sending me was being used for my personal needs. They also complained that I did not have theological knowledge and they wanted to advertise the position of the pastor in the local newspaper. The missions' coordinator, knowing that he had not been sending me any money and realizing these were just rumors, asked me whether I'd like to join Bible school.

I said I was ready for Bible school. I had been invited to Discipleship College by one pastor who was a student there and by this time he was lecturing in the same college. Therefore, I enrolled at the college where I have now been for five years. At the time I'm writing this story, I'm looking forward to graduating on November 26 with a degree through their collaboration partner, Chreso University.

To date the church has grown and we have constructed a church that can seat around 300 people. We have three other branches that have approximately 30 members each. My family has also grown. We have added a third child, a son named Ryan, which means 'small king' for he came when we were living better! I am now also chairman of the board of One Heart Children's Home which was started by our Australian partners. To God be the glory!

HIS GRACE IS SUFFICIENT
Paul Kipng'etich Cheboswony

Unfortunately, my mother, the fourth wife of my polygamous father, Cheboswony Kimasia, was barren. Even when I was born there was serious doubt that I would live, but I managed to survive. My father took great delight in my appearance on the scene. Our home was in Kokwet-Barsombe, Uasin Gishu District, Kenya.

My earliest memory was the time that my mom got saved. She loved the Lord very much and encouraged me and my brothers and sisters to attend Sunday School. I remember her drilling us in our memory verses and encouraging us to attend Sunday School. I was probably four years old at the time. I was an extremely shy child. My mother was a strong disciplinarian, so my fear of punishment followed me also to school where I feared the cane. But my childhood was happy. My mother supervised our study and was very concerned that we do well. Because she didn't have education, she was doubly determined that we would have an education and fear God. She repeated often, "Be educated and fear God."

I always went to Sunday School. The year I was in Standard 7 Christian university students came to our area to preach in an open air center. When they began to mingle with the crowd, one approached me and asked, "Are you saved?" I answered, "I'm going to Sunday School." He said, "That does not mean you are saved." He proceeded to lead me to Jesus Christ.

I excelled in school. In Standard 8 we were encouraged by our teachers to pass well so that we could attend Starehe Boys' School, a secondary school designed to help bright but poor students. Mom was alone at home caring for the cattle, etc., and therefore was often late preparing lunch. When I would reach home there was no lunch, so I

Tea Without Sugar: Chastened for a Destiny

decided to stay at school and not eat. That's when I started having physical problems. I contracted cerebral malaria which prevented me from taking KCPE (Kenyan Certificate of Primary Education) exams in 1992. I only did one paper, mathematics, on which I passed with an A. I was unable to do the rest. Consequently, I failed to make entrance to Starehe. However, I retried in 1993.

Instead of entering Starehe, however, God helped me to enter a very good Provincial school – Kabianga High School—one of the best schools in the country. Although my health was not good, I was able to attend most of the time. However, I was continually under medication. I came out with a C plain. A man who saw me in the hospital when I was sick told me that it was God who healed me, "so love God!" In secondary school, I found more time to study the Word so that I could love God more. I was active in the Christian Union. The head teacher commented that if I had had good health, I could have been leading the students that year. In poor health, I could obtain a C plain! He said that was equivalent to leading the students. I was, however, able to lead in another area. After high school, the African Inland Church appointed me to lead the youth in my local church. Later this leadership was it extended also to the district. I leaned more towards serving God, teaching Sunday School children and doing evangelism than following other pursuits.

But I was still weak in body. In fact, Mum was telling me that because of my health I shouldn't take those leadership responsibilities. However, I loved to do those things. When I moved out from the A.I.C. church, they commended my leadership efforts and said I was dedicated and determined.

It disturbed me greatly how young people my age in the church were behaving, because they were not living in the faith. The leaders of the youth were not setting a good example. When I became a leader, I was determined to bring change and set a good example. I developed a love for people who lived in peace with one another, who forgave each other. That passion has shaped my life.

My mother wanted my brothers and I to be circumcised in a Christian way, but my father, who was not saved, wanted us to be circumcised in a traditional way. What we had been taught in the Bible helped us to make a decision. In fact we used this verse, "We would

Tea Without Sugar: Chastened for a Destiny

rather obey God than man." When we made that decision, the community leaders tried to discourage us from being initiated in a Christian way. They told us the community might not accept us. In traditional circumcision there are covenants made by the boys which bind them to ancestral demonic forces. These rites make it very difficult after circumcision to reach young men in our community with the Gospel. Many become anti-Christian and resistant to the Gospel. I'm thankful my mother cautioned us and that we had the knowledge which helped us to obey God rather than man.

My church was not direct in telling me they couldn't help me, so I continued to pursue education with them. I was accepted by Moffat College of Bible, but my local church was not able to pay the fees. I waited for four years, but my decision came through a radio program. The preacher was saying, "There are vision killers. One is the people you live with. If you live among people who kill your vision, don't stay there." I decided to move to another denomination, Pentecostal.

I trusted God for money. I said, "I won't ask for money." A man named James Kimutai and his wife were sent by God to me. They were willing to help me attend Bible College. James had seen the signpost of Discipleship College and learned of the college through Milcah Birgen, a student, who had been invited to preach in a conference near our home. When James came I was far away from home taking care of family matters. In a dream, I saw James telling me to go to Discipleship and make application for entrance to the college. In my dream, there was a white person who gave me the application forms. The following day, I came home and mother said that James was looking for me. I went immediately to see him. He told me to go to Discipleship College in Pioneer and pick those application forms. When I came to pick the forms, Henry Lusala sent me to the office – and there was a white lady, Charlotte Russo, who gave me the application forms. My dream was being fulfilled.

I entered Discipleship College in May of 2004. James told his wife that they were willing to help me but financially they were not strong enough. He urged me, "Believe that God will provide." They did help me for one year and James' friends helped me after that. There were also scholarships from the school, donors who wanted to be unknown, and other friends who helped me. My mother occasionally helped as well, even though my father had passed away in 1999 and mother had the responsibility of educating other siblings in the university. There was little income for so many people, but she did her best. I was a Day Scholar while in college and actually many well wishers helped me. My brother helped me, though he had little income and was younger than me. But I often couldn't eat at noon. I struggled. That affected my health. But I used those times when I was not eating to pray and search the scriptures and my spirit was strengthened and it sustained me. This fasting helped me to do well in my studies. I became a spiritual leader in the college, especially in the area of prayer.

Long before college I had struggled with my church's position on the Holy Spirit. As I read scripture, particularly the book of Acts, I had many questions. "Why don't we speak in tongues," I asked. "The Bible speaks of it. When Peter and Paul filled were with the Holy Spirit they spoke in tongues." The response of one of the leaders was, "Do you want to get out of the church, Paul?" I said, "No, I just want to know why we don't see speaking in tongues in the AIC church." When we did discuss the issue, they explained it was not part of our beliefs because we didn't believe there are apostles now. Speaking in tongues was only for that time. But I desired that gift. I used to interact with others about it and I was longing for that experience. When I came to Discipleship College, the campus pastor, Pastor Andrew Russo was organizing *keshas* (overnight prayer vigil services) at night. We used to pray and he always encouraged those among us who had not yet been baptized with the Holy Spirit that it was a blessing we could experience. I was one of those who longed to experience the infilling of the Holy Spirit, but it took time.

My time came during a chapel service. There was a student speaking about being endued with power by the Holy Spirit. Afterwards, the campus pastor invited those who wanted to be filled with the Spirit to come forward. We were five who responded. I experienced something I had never experienced before. I spoke in tongues and was so filled with God's presence that I remained in the chapel for some time. My ministry was transformed. We continued to experience His presence in the *night keshas*. I never missed one of those gatherings. I received frequent visions and had a new boldness.

After I had preached, people would say that it was as if someone had told me what was happening and I was ministering to that need. I experienced the guidance of the Holy Spirit in a new way. One time I heard a voice in my mind telling me to go see Jeanette Chesser (a visiting adjunct faculty). I was afraid because students were not allowed to go to the faculty residences. But the voice repeated the command three times so I decided it was the leading of the Holy Spirit. When I visited her I received a second filling. It was like the weight of the glory of the Lord fell upon me. I was facing many challenges and I was given a gift of faith to do the impossible for myself, personally and in my ministry. My outlook on life changed dramatically. God spoke through her the following, "You are not given the name Paul in vain, when you stand tall you are spiritually tall, crowds will be under you, to listen to what God is speaking. I will make you known in this land. (This was repeated) You will go through sufferings. But I will give you knowledge and wisdom." This word greatly encouraged me.

Another defining moment came in a time of conflict. I was called to make a decision against the views of the majority. I stood against them because I knew in my spirit that God was not in favor of what they were doing. That decision made me stand out from the others. Before that I was unknown. Standing in my faith, made me became a leader and I found myself in the gap between two groups. There was one group of the majority and one of the few. Eventually, I joined the few. The following day there was a *baraza* (a community council meeting) to solve the conflict. I was not quick in speaking. The meeting was ending and the question was asked, "Who still has a word." There was a prompting in my heart, but I was afraid. It was like someone was raising me up. When God urged me to speak, it was from Matthew 5:9: *Blessed are the peacemakers for they will be called the sons of God.* I told them that God would exalt the humble and humble the proud. They were not my words. They were His. The director concluded the meeting saying that there was a spirit of rebellion at work. For sure the majority were greatly humbled. Their union broke and we began to see progress come towards unity at the College. Afterwards I was put in spiritual leadership in the college. One of the faculty told me that the lecturers honored me because of my godly stand on matters.

The director encouraged us as students to minister at small, local churches. I went to an AIC church in Kipkaren. A revival came in that small church. There was a baptism class which had stopped for some reason and the pastor asked me to restart it. I was able to follow their program, but to expand on the section about the Holy Spirit. One of the students in gratitude paid my fees at Discipleship. A revival came in that group and a prayer group was started. They even wanted me to become the pastor but I declined.

At this point the opportunity came for me to begin a work in Kabarnet. The director of Discipleship College, Gordon Bloodworth, told me that someone had given land in Baringo for a church. Jeanette Chesser told me afterwards that she had told Gordon she knew the man that was going to go there. Later Gordon said in class, "We need a man to go from the Kalenjin community." I told him I was willing to go. Another student had also said he would go, but later he said that he wife would not go there. Jeanette shared that God had showed her that I would be the one. Our faculty member, Judy Karei, was burdened because she had seen how many young people were drunk there. When she shared this with Magdalene from Nigeria, Magdalene said, "God will send a zealous young man to preach in that place." When I went there I targeted the drunkards. Among them was a young man who later became my "Timothy," who currently pastors the church I pioneered.

It is amazing how God has worked in the life of my *Timothy** convicting and converting him. God has blessed him with a job, blessed him spiritually, emotionally, and mentally through the Certificate in Ministerial Studies program. There were many who heard, but many lacked full commitment. I am urging this *Timothy* of mine to follow them up.

I have seen that it was the Holy Spirit who sent me to Kabarnet. I was discouraged by many from going there. Within me, my driving force was to reach the unreached. When I began going there, there were resources for one month. After that, the campus pastor had an idea that the students could contribute every Thursday for my going to Kabarnet. So the mission began. Every week I needed money for fare, food and a place to sleep. Sometimes I slept in the church.

Finally, one man in Kabarnet saw my struggles and offered a place to stay in his house. His name was Hillary Kiptarus. Though he belonged to another denomination, he had a "kingdom mentality" and was a great help to me. I stayed at his home every time I went to Kabarnet until I finished at Discipleship College. Two times groups from Discipleship College came to minister. The first group was students from the school, the second was the evangelistic team, Eagles Wings.

This ministry was characterized by perseverance and patience. I remember a time when the money I had to return to college was only enough to go to Iten. From Iten I walked to Eldoret.** God was separating me to serve. I rejoiced in my suffering. My joy was in reaching the people, especially the children and drunkards.

Afterwards the CIMS program began. A man had planted a church but was not able to establish it fully. He admired my education and wanted my college to bring training to Kabarnet. Gordon said, "If there are two we will give you the books and you can begin." I thought that my Timothy could study with the first man. When I took books for those two, there were four others who were interested as well. I requested for more books. The first course was Old Testament Survey. These people came from different churches, one from New Testament Church of God, one from Deliverance Church, one from Christian Worship and one from AIC. While these people were continuing with the course, the content so blessed them that they were sharing with others. Others wanted to join, but I told them to wait until the next course, knowing the Holy Spirit. By this time there was an increase to 12 students. Some of the students who were interested were not strong financially. Because I was traveling, I could understand hardship. I had been helped to study myself and I was moved with compassion. I encouraged them to continue. In fact what I saw was the need to empower these people for what they would do in the future. I didn't focus much on the fees for those who were not able. If they at least were able to pay the college for the book, I encouraged them to continue. As I had been helped I wanted to help others. There were others who came but dropped on the way. The number eventually grew to 22 students in total. Some are still working to finish the CIMS program.

Apart from doing evangelism and training, other opportunities for me to minister were opened. Students at the Christian Union of a medical college, students in 3 primary schools and staff and workers of the School for the Deaf and the Blind received my ministry. God opened many doors. I also visited the prisons and ministered both to the officers and the prisoners. Churches opened their doors to me for lunch hour ministry. Pastors often invited me to teach their congregation then without fear of my stealing sheep! I was ready to be a tentmaker, but I could not get a job. I applied to three schools, but the doors were closed because I was from a different area. Their priority was the people in that particular district. In many closed areas such as this, people will even demonstrate on the streets when a job is given to an outsider.

I am a farmer, but that area is not a farming area. My skills didn't match with theirs. I am not good in business. Paul could make tents, but what I knew how to do I couldn't practice there. The church was small and growing, but people were struggling to pay rent and school fees and therefore could not support me. If I challenged them to help pay the rent, they would stay home. Most of the finances were used for rent and paying bills of the church, and secondly for me to eat and be clothed. Consequently, I was often ill. Thankfully, my family often helped me and other people were moved by God to help me. Once, my students, who came from other denominations, paid four months' rent for the church. Unfortunately, there is not a structure for support of new churches in any district of New Testament Church of God at this point.

There was a time when I felt so pressured that I wanted to leave. I was sick and had a lot of debts. My mentor said, to me, "Go ahead and go home, but remember, it is God who sent you there." I was challenged and encouraged and asked God to help me. What burdened me most was the CIMS course that we had just begun. I knew that it must continue. I was afraid to be a bad example. One student was told by God the very next morning to give me 3,000 Kenya shillings and the students began to pay for their courses and beyond. So the debt was paid, and there was 1,000 extra. I continued by God's grace. God provided. I saw his providence. My students have learned a lot from the books, but also through my struggles, how I feared God, and how I could hang on in spite of many difficulties

While visiting in a home, I viewed a DVD called Women of Faith. While I was watching a word came to my heart, "This can happen in Kabarnet." I wrote this in my notebook, "Women of Faith: United in God's Love, Sisters By Grace." I decided to share with two women students the idea that they, as women, could be used to be a blessing to the town by spear-heading that ministry. I shared with Naomi Kimetto and Naomi Sawe strategies of how to reach women's leaders of other denominations to ignite them with the vision. I suggested that they pray together, sharing this vision to organize a meeting of women throughout Kabarnet. They prayed about it, called other women and wrote a banner in the town about the meeting. The first speakers were Dr. Marcia Anderson and Juddy Karei from Discipleship. Juddy shared her own powerful testimony about how God had healed her and given her a vision as a woman to impact her community. Marcia challenged the women to be "Nathan's" who are able to "care-front" (gently confront) others – even leaders - who have broken relationships in the Body of Christ. There was a tremendous move of the Holy Spirit as first these women themselves were healed in areas of broken relationships and then yielded themselves to be used to influence their community and help bring about unity in the churches. God had begun a continuing ministry, which meets monthly. The pastors of the town are very impressed and thankful. They are saying, "God bless the one who thought to begin this." Through the CIMS program, students became leaders and catalysts for unity in the city. That gathering was the first interdenominational meeting ever held in the city.

Now the men are jealous. They plan to meet in January. Those who attended the CIMS program, have seen the women have done something and they want to be a blessing also.

When the first CIMS class completed its course, I knew that my work was finished there. I had shared years before with Jeanette Chesser about my heart is to reach Moslems. She had encouraged me to wait on God, that He would use me in the meantime in other areas until the time would be right for me to work with Moslems. He would be preparing me for that special work. It was now time for me to start to focus more specifically on how to minister to this unreached people group. People did not want me to leave Kabarnet, but I knew that it was time. Our director used to say, "When God stops providing, He does not need you there." I told them I wanted to go and study. Noel Kipruto, my "Timothy" organized a farewell and I prepared for my transition. I am seeking God's direction and timing for launching out in that ministry. I know that many of the experiences in Kabarnet have prepared me for this next step. The Apostle Paul said in 2 *Corinthians 12:9: And He has said to me, "My grace is sufficient for you, for power is perfected in weakness." Most gladly, therefore, I will rather boast about my weaknesses, that the power of Christ may dwell in me.*

>*Paul sees Noel as his *Timothy*, in the same way that the apostle Paul invested his life and effort to disciple Timothy in the Bible.
>**A distance of 35 kilometers

EXPELLED TO EXCEL
Lawrence Ouma Osewe

I have always been interested in writing my story, so that people will realize that it is not the background of a person that determines his destiny. As a young child I would often dream of standing before huge crowds, speaking and praying for them.

My name is Lawrence Ouma. I was born in the year 1974, February, in a family of 11. I was the 9th born son of my dad who had been trusting that "this time" there would be a girl. Finally, after me, came two girls. My own father never wanted to be close to me. I never experienced paternal love. At the time of my birth my father had just married his second wife. That marriage brought a lot of hostility into the family. Soon after marrying the second wife, he sent my mom back to the village with me, so that he could focus on the second wife. There were just six months between me and the first child of the second marriage. I was raised by my mum and it came to my realization only when I was around 10 years old that most people lived with their fathers. When people talked about their fathers, it was like a story to me.

I grew up in a cruel situation that really made me have bitterness in my heart. In the year 1986 my dad retired and came back home to join us. By that time the whole family had come back, including the step-brothers. There was never peace between me and the other boys. My father hated me most, perhaps because I was the most outspoken. This caused me to develop a negative attitude towards the other boys. After all, I wasn't a stepchild. I was his own child. When I reached Standard Seven in 1990, one of my brothers decided to take me to stay in Kitale.

From a religious point of view, we were raised in a staunch Catholic family. I went through baptism, first communion and confirmation, but all those rituals did not bring meaning into my life.

In Kitale I attended a crusade. There was a team of preachers who had come from London. I was sick. That was the first time in my life to hear about the gospel. After I listened, I believed and was healed. My life changed. After the crusade, I walked with the Lord for one year but attended no church. Having had no discipling, it was, I suppose, not surprising that when I finished my Class Eight the next year, I back-slid. I became a very bad boy. I joined Cherangani High School in Kitale. The Christian Union was very active and quite often I was convicted to surrender back my life to the Lord but I was not ready for it. Instead, I got involved in acts of hooliganism, and participated in a series of strikes which landed me in a law court. Because I told them everything, the truth, though it was very risky for me, I was re-instated in school. All my colleagues were expelled from the school, but I was able to continue with my learning. When the time came for me to enroll as a candidate for the KCSE (Kenyan Certificate of Secondary Education), I got myself into problems with the school again and I was expelled just two days before the exams.

After being expelled, I was forced to do my exams from outside the school. My brother, who was acting as my guardian, abandoned me. But the Lord intervened. He brought a Good Samaritan. Someone provided a house for me and everything else I needed while I took my exams. I remember one afternoon when the exams were going on – when I was just about to finish the exams – the headmaster conspired with other members of the teaching staff to prevent me from finishing. One person came to provoke me, thinking that I would fight back. When I didn't respond violently, he ordered the watchman to chase me out of the school. I went away. In fact, I had given up. I thought, "This is the end of my education." But when I reached the outside the school, I happened to meet a policemen and the supervisors of the exams. I told them what was going on. After hearing my story, they pointed out that the headmaster could not prevent me from finishing my exams once I had enrolled. I was encouraged and I came back to school. When I returned, I found my desk had been taken. I quietly took one of the chairs of the supervisors and continued writing my exams until I had finished.

After finishing Form Four, I went back home and began doing business. The business I engaged in was illegal. I started smuggling ivory across the Ugandan and Tanzanian borders. My family was opposed to my doing that kind of business to the point that my dad disowned me. He did not want to see me around. But down deep inside of my heart, I used to cry. I would sit down to look at the way things were going, but I did not fully understand how things were going in my life. I felt I needed divine intervention again. I had tasted it, but had lost my way. So, I continued with the business, though it was very risky. I remember several times when we narrowly escaped from policemen. I came very close to being arrested. It was indeed a dangerous business. One night, in 1990, I was conned of everything in the middle of Nairobi. This business was not helping me in any way.

Several years later, in 1998, I stopped drinking alcohol. I said in my heart, "I want to be very sober. I want to think about my life." I remember that time I had traveled home during Christmas holidays. I'll never forget what my dad said to me, "Even if you die, I won't have lost anything." That word really pierced my heart. In the beginning of 1999, I started the year in the church in an organized prayer meeting. Though I never wanted anything to do with the church, I found myself there. When I heard people preach, the conviction was very strong, but I was not willing to surrender. Instead, I went back to the same business, going to Uganda again. This time around, I remember that upon our return trip, our vehicle was stopped by the police. We had just bought some ivory. The police searched everyone in the vehicle and I was the one carrying it. The policeman just looked at me and didn't touch anything that I was carrying. He simply allowed us to continue with the journey.

It was about two days later that we arrived in Kitale. A preacher from Nairobi had come to town. He was playing music which caused me to be attracted to the meeting. The Word of God touched my life in that meeting. That evening I came under great conviction but had not surrendered everything, though I knew I needed to. The next day I was in the house alone. I heard someone telling me, "You need to surrender your life," so I knelt down and made a very short prayer. When I finished praying, I realized I was now able to see how truly lost I had been. I realized how stupid I had been. At the same time, I began to feel some kind of joy and peace. I went back again to the crusade to hear more teaching. Now I had surrendered everything in my life except my girl friend in Nairobi. I left the place, determined finally to release everything. I went to the office and my girl friend called from Nairobi. She asked me, "Where were you? I've been calling you." I told her I was in the crusade. She said, "It's not the time to be at a crusade. Your voice has changed." I told her, "I've given my life to Jesus, and abandoned everything, including you." She laughed. I ended the call. And that is how our relationship ended.

Two days after my conversion, I heard the Lord speak to me in an audible voice. "You have to go back to your homeland and witness to My people in Kisumu." I gave him very genuine excuses. I told him, "I do not know how to speak. I am a private man, not a public figure. There is no spiritual church in my homeland. I don't know how to pray. There is not one youth who is born again." After that, a rumor came into the town, that the preacher who just preached to us at the crusade was killed in Nairobi. I felt so bad. I said that if Silvanus Aoko has gone to be with the Lord, I will take over his ministry. I looked for a Bible. I was reading my Bible throughout the day. I stopped my friendship with other boys. I was going to a prayer meeting every day at lunch time. After two days, I heard the Lord telling me, "You must go and witness to my people." Again, I told God, "I will not go." The next Sunday, I attended Deliverance Church, which I felt was a spiritual church. On Monday, when I left the house going to my work place, thieves came. They opened the door, took all our money, plus things in the house. They stole the money I was using for business and the stuff we had just bought in Uganda. I remembered a song I heard about the perils of smuggling. I had already abandoned 400,000 ksh to my partner and had decided that I must start afresh. I didn't want one cent from that business. Now the spirit of God was asking me, "What if you should be arrested again?"

I decided to leave for home, as the Lord was ordering me to do, though it was not my wish. When I reached Kisumu town, I decided to go on to Migori town where one of my brothers resided. When He found me reading the Bible and realized that I was saved, he told me, "You have to go home. You can't stay with me." So the next day I went back home where God wanted me to be. The response of my family was positive. My mom and dad were happy, but my father did not believe that I was truly converted. He thought maybe I was just trying to pretend. I stayed for one week. People were inviting me to go and speak to them because I was someone that was known. The administration of the province was happy that I was now converted. God had now helped them to see me in a different way. I joined a PEFA church (Pentecostal Evangelistic Fellowship of Africa) of three people. All of them were old people. The pastor received me with a lot of joy. During one of their meetings, my life changed completely. I received the Baptism of the Holy Spirit, just two weeks after I had been born again. I began to do ministry on a serious note. People were calling me to their homes. I was praying for them. People were getting saved. In a short time, the church that was almost dead was revived.

Yes, revival came to that church. Young men – drug addicts, alcoholics, thieves – were saved and their lives were transformed. Everybody was happy about the church. The chief of the area once told us we could pray all night because he had seen how people's lives were being transformed. The revival did not end there. It spread to the other neighboring churches. Other churches were planted during that move of God and produced many servants of God. I served for around four years in the village and the impact was great. God moved. People were healed, barren women gave birth, prayer campaigns were organized for community deliverance, and fasting occurred to address communal problems that were facing us. As a result God brought judgment that wiped away the witch doctors in that area. God restored many people. God was moving with mighty manifestations until the leaders started becoming jealous.

I began feeling the urge to go back to school. I shared this desire with my pastor. He tried to find a place for me in Nairobi Pentecostal Bible College. The overseer and my pastor, however, were not on good terms. The forms which I was to get from the overseer somehow weren't given me. I knew I hadn't maximized the potential that was in me in my high school years. I really wanted to use my abilities to the full. But, because of this disappointment, I lost my vision for furthering my studies.

After that I gave up the idea of joining college. I was being told that now I needed to marry, but I was not convicted in that direction. One of the pastors who was a friend called me. He knew the kind of ministry God had placed in my heart. He wanted to plant a church for me. He was aware of my frustration, so I accepted. We found a good venue and he financed the whole meeting. But, as the meeting was going on, my heart was not at peace. On the last Sunday morning, after our 4 am morning devotion, a brother followed me out of the service and told me there was something he wanted to share with me. This was Brother Cornell Ochieng, who was a student at Discipleship College. He told me, "There is no hurry in ministry. Have you ever thought to further your studies?" I told him, "That is what I've always wanted." Immediately, I began experiencing peace in my heart again. He told me that he had been in a college in Eldoret for one year and had experienced great changes in his ministry. He told me I should not be in a hurry doing ministry, that I should be equipped. I was convinced then and there.

After that I told that pastor that if it is God's will, then I'll pastor this church, but if it is not God's will, I will not pastor it. "Give me one month." The pastor was very angry and abused me. But my decision stood. Brother Cornell gave me all the contacts for Discipleship. I met with Brother Gordon Bloodworth and we talked together. I was admitted. After being given admission I was not sure how I was going to make it in terms of school fees. I went back home and discussed it with my family. They agreed to support me for one term. After that term, my struggles began again. I had to begin trusting God in a greater way. I struggled with my parents for one year. They managed to see me through that one year, but they then abandoned me because they could not see that what I was doing would benefit them. My going to a theological college could not benefit them financially.

I remember one semester I was sent home because I had no money for school fees. I locked myself in a room and prayed. I could not understand what was going on. God showed me in a vision that He would provide for me, but I did not know how it would happen. That was 2004.

In 2005, I didn't even have transport fare to Eldoret, let alone the fees. I was left alone. I remember I told God, "I never knelt down and asked to come to Eldoret, but you opened the door Yourself. Since you opened that door, you finish it." There was a lady in

Eldoret, a friend of my room-mate, who was seriously interested in me. When I told her I was not coming back to Eldoret, she encouraged me to reconsider and she said she would support me. She paid for three courses, but I had to look for a place outside campus to live. I found a house, not too far away, in Langas, for which she paid the rent. She also bought me a few things so I could come back to school again. The balance from the previous year was still pending and I did not know how it would be cleared. One day Gordon said, "If you have a balance, you will not take your exams." I went home, packed my things, and said, "God has failed. Let me go home and structure my life again." Brother Gordon had said those who had balances would have their names put on the notice board. So I went to look for my name, but I did not find it there. I thought it must be a computer error. I was waiting to see what would happen. Charlotte Russo called me into the office and told me someone had paid off all my balance. I repented – I had said God had failed. I was wrong. I tried to find out who had paid my fees. Later on she told me who it was. I looked for Jeanette Chesser's email and told her thanks. She told me it was God who had ordered her to do that. She promised to continue to support me to help me finish my education. I was forced to look for a job, so that I could pay for other things. I got a job at a school called Blossom. I worked there for one year while doing external studies. I was not able to attend classes because of the time schedule. I worked until I finished. Finally, I graduated. During my graduation, I called my family to inform them. They were amazed. No, perhaps shocked is a better description of their reaction. They didn't think that I would make it.

Since 2003, I had been in a church called Christian Growth Center. There the doors to do ministry were locked. I was gifted, I had the ministry in me, but it was never allowed to be used. I was wasted in the church for 6 years. After 6 years I went to tell the pastor, "I will not sit down any longer." He gave me opportunity to preach one Sunday in all the services. That preaching was the first and the last. He was discouraging me by saying that preaching revival would kill me.

Brother Reuben Riang'a was getting ready to go to the US to study, so I joined the church he pastored, Christ the Rebuilder, thinking

I could help there. I stayed in Eldoret for one year without support. But the Lord saw me through. Once my house was locked by the landlord and I slept outside because I was not able to pay the rent. My relationship never worked with the lady who had supported me. She abandoned me. I did not want to plead with her. Later the Lord opened a door for me to work at FISH Media (Fishing for the Lost and Feeding the Found). There I served, doing ministry and also doing some administration. I remember that in that office God brought people to me. Every day people got saved and many were being healed.

In 2002 I had proposed to another lady. It took her two years to give me a "no" answer. After that we did not communicate for 3 years. In 2007 I went to look for her again. She did not want to marry a minister. I found the Lord had dealt with Linet Akinyi's life. At that time I was working at Blossom. This time she accepted my proposal. We courted for some time up to 2009. We were planning for a wedding, but when I was unable to complete preparations, she left again. In 2010 January, we finally married.

In 2011 I went back to the church that raised me – to a Pentecostal Evangelical Fellowship church in West Campus, Eldoret. Now, I'm looking forward to launching an evangelistic ministry from that church, something that will go all over the country. My father now respects me and asks me for prayer, especially for healing. I now have a baby daughter, whom I named after Jeanette Chesser, the mentor who inspired me and stood with me. Through her obedience to the Lord I was able to finish at Discipleship College. To God be the glory!

TIL DEATH DO US PART: OUR STORY

FloJo Sikobe

Today is the 31st day of October, 2015 at 3pm. Florence and John are seated together at the entrance to their home in East Elgon-view Estate, Eldoret. We are taking in vitamin D, courtesy of the hot tropical sun so generously looking down on us.

BUT, Florence is seated in a wheel-chair because both legs are weak and she is unable to move her right side. She can only look at the world from the confines of a wheel chair. She looks around but cannot make a sound because her speech has been lost. After five strokes and other afflictions Flo has experienced great physical suffering. Now paralyzed and completely dependent on others for survival her physical appearance is a far cry from that girl I first met in a bus in Nairobi. Our Christian walk has been punctuated by the challenges of poor health but with God's redeeming favor we have stood.

The Meeting

Our story begins in 1976 when we first met in a Kenya Bus Service (KBS) bus from Mariakani Estate, South B going into the CBD of Nairobi City early in the morning. The meeting was electrifying for me! I beheld a most beautiful creation of a lady clad in a great outfit, donning a wonderful natural Afro hairdo and wearing one of the cutest dimpled smiles framed by a smooth skinned face that I had ever seen. I was enthralled, captivated and enchanted all at once. No wonder I could not help but stare at her with mouth agape! Rude and ungentlemanly as it was, I could not help myself.

Tea Without Sugar: Chastened for a Destiny

The workings of God in life are strange indeed. When we pray for His divine intervention we look to His answers with hope, yet at times with bated breath. For me, in that bus, that morning in an instant my prayer for a wife had been answered. Looking at her for the very first time my heart was aglow with the expectation of a friendship, a love engagement and a blossoming into "I, John, take thee Florence to be my wedded wife." Ooooh! It felt so wonderful to be unexpectedly love-struck that morning.

Beginnings for John

I was born into the Sikobe family in Kericho on 30th March 1955 as child number two. Kericho has always been to me a county that demonstrates how beautiful God's creation can be. The undulating hills are covered with carpet-like tea bushes. They are quite a sight to behold and indeed carry with them romantic imagery. My older brother was called Lincoln. He was a great older brother whose boxing skills came to my rescue many a time against bigger boys and bullies. He died after a short illness in the late sixties. My siblings after me are Nicholas, Anne and Christopher. Our parents Shadrack Ouya and Miriam Wanjiku Sikobe were dedicated to caring for us. Theirs was a marriage of determined love that crossed tribal boundaries. Having met at the Royal King George Hospital (now Kenyatta National Referral Hospital) their declared love for each other took their parents by surprise and met with immediate resistance and rejection due to the tribal factor. My father was a Luhya from Western Kenya who was seen by my maternal grandparents as unsuitable for my Kikuyu mother. On the other hand, my mother, was considered equally unsuitable and a great risk, since my father's parents knew that children in Kikuyu culture belong to the mother. That Luhya couple could not countenance the idea that in a situation of marital differences she might run away with their grandchildren.

My early memories at home include a brief stay in Bunyore, Western Kenya, in classes one and two. After resigning his job at the Kericho District Hospital where he had worked as a compounder in the pharmacy, my father moved to the capital city, Nairobi. Meanwhile he had moved us to live with our grandparents.

When my dad finally found both a job and a house in 1964 that could accommodate us, he sent for us to join him in Nairobi. My impressions of the train ride to the city and my encounter with what appeared to be innumerable number of lights in very tall buildings and even on the streets was like a Disneyland experience. My legs walked but my eyes would not look down to provide direction. My eyes were glued to the skies as I surveyed the tall structures while wondering about my safety in-case they came tumbling down.

This experience was too much for a nine year old boy from the village. The very fact that I was in Nairobi after a long train ride was itself unbelievable; a dream come true! The steam engine locomotive had always held a fascination for us kids. Smoke spewing into the sky, it snaked through valleys and hills on its way to far away destinations. The engine noise and the wheels seemed to sing rhythmically with every meter of forward movement. How we dreamt of going to that place where the train goes. Now, finally, my dream had been realized and I had found the place where the train goes.

The village had opened me up to the Gospel through the Sunday School activities at the local Church of God at Epang'a. I fondly recollect teacher Robai, the Sunday School teacher leading us in the song: "Let us go to Sunday School, Sunday School, Sunday School. Let us go to Sunday all the children come." Madam Robai had a lifelong effect on me as even in later life I just could not forget the joy she brought to my little spirit during her lessons. She went to be with the Lord at a ripe old age above ninety_but s. She had never lost her contagious smile and love for the Lord even in old age. Oh praise the Lord!

The city was a great place to grow up. The social amenities were available with plenty of open fields to enjoy football and other games. Our home was flat number 222 in Block M, at Mariakani Estate, Nairobi South B. It was reasonably comfortable with three bedrooms in a very well kept and clean estate. Use of charcoal in this estate was forbidden and the level of cleanliness maintained by the City Council was impeccable.

We grew up in the sixties and seventies when gangs formed a major part of social interaction amongst the youth. Every estate or city locality seemed to have a youth gang that 'ruled' and 'protected' their turf jealously. The gangs provided a sense of belonging for many of us and also shielded us from other groups that would harm us.

The 'boogie' or daylight disco dances and occasional night parties provided entertainment. Occasionally some youth would bring along alcohol, cigarettes and weed (*cannabis sativa*). But it has always been a point of thanksgiving for me how the Lord protected me from developing an appetite for these substances and kept me relatively free from them. Some of my friends were not so lucky.

Our parents insisted that we should attend Church at the Mariakani Christian Centre run by Church of God in East Africa. Our Christian experience there was a little lukewarm except for the games and other physical activities that were open to us at the church. As we became teenagers, our attention was grabbed by overwhelming peer pressure to conform to the escapades of our age-mates outside the Church.

I soon found myself elected the Chairman of the gang then known as MASOBRA (an acronym for **MA**riakani, **SO**uth B, **RA**ilways). Our main activities included football, karate, boxing and judo. Extra entertainment took the form of parties and boogies. When not doing these activities we were generally hanging out and 'beating' stories. Part of the duties the chairman performed was the official opening of all dances and parties. This was always done with what seemed to be much relish. Leadership at whatever stage in life appears to draw a sense of responsibility besides the feeling of attainment. This peer recognition soothes the ego somehow and drives one on to greater attainment. But even that, I soon found out, could not satisfy the inner longing and had to serve some serious purpose in my life. The emptiness in my spirit could not be filled with these mundane attainments of youth. Coming out at the top of the pile of one's peers did not come with a long lasting satisfaction. It became clear that there must be something deeper that one can live for.

Schooling in Nairobi was fun. My brothers, Lincoln and Nicholas, and I attended St. Peter Clavers Primary School from 1964 to 1968. It required that we take a bus ride from South B to the main bus station and walk the short distance to the school. There were times when we would walk all the way and spend the bus-fare at 'Uplands of Course' pork goodies (Now Farmer's Choice). St. Peter's was a Catholic school and we at times participated in the services. However, there was never any attachment developed to that worship style. We transferred to Khalsa Primary School in neighboring South C in the last term of class five and I took my KCPE (Kenyan Certificate of Primary Education) in class seven in 1968.

In 1969 I joined Lord Delamere High School (Now Upper Hill School) in Nairobi for 'O' Level education. It was also a football playing school, so I was soon enrolled to play for the school team. It was an O and A level school and had great success in football. I made it to the school 's first Eleven while in Form 3 and football seemed to be a great part of my life. In the national schools edition in 1971/2 we went to represent Nairobi Province at the Shimo La Tewa High School, Mombasa. The contest was very hot and animosity developed into violence between coastal students and the brash Nairobians. We were attacked by the Shimo boys while asleep in the dorms and the Police had to come and rescue us. We slept at the Police Station for our own safety.

At Upper Hill, I had my first encounter with the Christian Union. I just could not understand how young guys could spend time in CU services singing and listening to preaching. However, I was fascinated by the demeanor of the CU leader brother Muyela who appeared to be so collected, sober and holy. But it was not until I joined Kericho High School in 1973 for my A Levels that the CU and its members became a very real challenge to my life.

Before going to join Kericho for my A Levels, my dear mother died in March, 1973 at the Kenyatta National Hospital after a long battle with hypertension. Thank God for my father who helped steer the family firmly back onto the road to recovery. I always felt close to my mother and knew she had been the glue that kept the family together. However, our father came through for us in this crisis in a magnificent manner.

Kericho High School presented me my first experience of what boarding life was like. Joining Form 5 for my A Levels I was intrigued by my new found life away from home. It allowed very much freedom away from home and gave me the opportunity to begin maturing a little too fast. My reputation was not very good. Being from Nairobi, I was considered to be a little 'mukora' (crook-ish). It did not help my reputation at all when I took the role of leading the boys to the

Kipsigis Girls High School every weekend to visit with the girls. One thing that I held close to my heart was the desire never to disrespect the sisters. Being a romantic, I seemed to enjoy treating the sisters like ladies. You could say that I was a gentleman of some sort! Eric Oyondi Nganyi (now Dr. Eric Oyondi Nganyi, University lecturer) and I also started a Karate instruction class in the school to instruct willing students. I was not the kind of guy many students wanted to mess with.

The School management appointed me as the captain responsible for Abosi House, which was one of four dormitories in the school. This helped lift my level of responsibility and reduced the possible waywardness that could have been manifested in my stay at Kericho. Besides football one of my highlights at Kericho was when in 1973 I participated in and won the Family Planning Society of Kenya's National Essay Competition. My English teacher was very elated by my performance which came with a top prize of Kshs. 500/= (Five Hundred Only). Back in 1973, this could have paid almost one month's rent in our Nairobi Council three bedroom flat at Mariakani Estate! That was something.

During the year 1973 my preoccupation with being 'macho' would not allow me to seriously consider a commitment as a Christian. How could one purport to follow Jesus whilst still embracing a thoroughly secular and sinful lifestyle? The desire to be accepted by those that made up our peers was overwhelming because that was the only way we, as youth, thought that life must be lived. Looking at the Christian Union crowd we saw a people that were boring and who did not seem to know how to enjoy life.

God works in mysterious ways! Right there in the same class with me was the CU Chairman designate. He was due to take over after the Form 6 A level class of 1973 finished their exams in November. His name was Norbetus and he had an infectious laugh and joy when he spoke about the Lord Jesus. His faith seemed so real and personal that it got me wondering if there was indeed some serious truth in the Gospel. Maybe something that had remained hidden from me?

On the 15th January 1974 we reported back to school to begin our Form 6, A Level studies. Many of us gathered in the dormitory to receive updates on our holiday exploits. The first night of term was always a most exciting time of lively exchanges of stories. Sleeping was delayed to allow everyone who needed to speak to do so. The discussion somehow flowed into religion and faith. By the end of the discussion I found myself having answered yes to the question of salvation: Do you want to be saved? At about 9.30pm John Sikobe had chosen Christ as Lord and Savior of his life! It was unbelievable and quite unexpected, but it was fact. Praise the Lord!The news of my salvation took the students by surprise. Most did not believe it and gave me just two weeks to backslide into my old ways. But God is merciful, now we are in 2015 and He has kept me.

Friendship: The Blade that Sharpens Life's Experiences

It is early 1976, the month and day are unclear. It is in the evening and three young people can be seen walking in the lower Mariakani Estate gardens. They are visibly animated as they engage in deep discussion about life. The discussions cover dreams and aspirations for the future. They relive the days' experiences and just hangout and 'chapa' (tell) stories. Loud laughter rings out as they enjoy their discussion. These evening walks had become a daily ritual for relaxing. The Swahili expression was, 'ku poa' implying a cooling down, a slowing down of the day's clock of activity when they took stock of their import.

Sometimes (seemed like almost all the time) these walks would be punctuated by a brief stop-over at Block D. This was so as to allow one of the young men to say hallo to a beautiful maiden. The lass had smitten the heart of the lad and like in those epic battles of conquest, had taken it away with her, and held it captive deep in the prison of her own heart. Those interruptions to the walk were always welcome and their timing and frequency were suspiciously premeditated. These walks were forming the foundation upon which the future of these young men would unfold.

Now let us fast forward to Tuesday, 19th January 2016, a whole forty years later and the scene has changed. It is a day like any other, the scene remains Nairobi, Kenya, but this time the location is deep in the Karen suburbs in an imposing mansion, the same 'young' men are seated around in a room. They are young because even after forty years, they can declare with Caleb, 'Give me that mountain.' You can clearly see that the ravages of aging have been held back with the gracious preservation of youth by their Maker. The glimmer of comradeship remains, and also the fierce burning of hearts that now fully comprehend with hindsight how gracious, how good God Almighty has been to them over the years of their lives.

In the middle of the room a 'girl' lies on a double bed. This is the same 'girl' who in 1976 had conquered the heart of one of the young men. She has a smile on her face. That face still carries the irresistible beauty of yester years. The hair is long and naturally attractive. Her look is coy; a picture of innocence. Life has been good to her. God has preserved her and seen her through many a challenge. He has also given her the experience of great joy and love: experiences that make every bitter challenge seem like a feathery slap on her face.

Five strokes and other challenges notwithstanding, this 'girl' continues to tenaciously and resolutely hold onto the faith she first professed back on 23rd September 1977 at Mariakani South B, shopping centre at a rally led by Pastor Francis Suza.

Reminiscing on days gone by, these 'young' men who are now grandparents remind each other of how God has been faithful and kept them over the years. They are amazed by what is now obvious to them; God had a plan for their lives after all! They can see God's hand in their affairs even though it may not have been very visible those early days.

Names begin to pop up from memory. Names of those friends and youth members whose lives were forever changed due to the interaction they had at Mariakani Christian Centre, South B. Their recall of activities and events reveal that their friendship was special in many ways. Their friendship has sharpened them as they engaged each other concerning their dreams and aspirations for life. This friendship was used to challenge each other to make meaningful outcomes of their lives. Just like iron sharpens iron, another man sharpens the other through the experiences of friendship.

Here they are, after forty years, seated in that room for the first time all of them together! They surround this precious 'girl' on the bed, and each hold back the spackle of a tear, the expression of awe and wonder written on their faces. It clearly dawns on them that God used their friendship to help them come to this place in this room. Their declaration is made in unison as they consider God's part in their lives: 'On Christ the solid rock I stand, all other ground is sinking sand, all other ground is sinking sand.' Oh the wonder of God's faithfulness. His plans for us are for our good to bring us to a desired end and purpose.

A circle has been formed around the 'girl' on the bed. Patrick Muindi Mutua continues to hold her left hand caringly, while Beverly Omido warmly holds her right hand, Babu Omido holds Beverly by his left hand while his right hand holds Nick Sikobe, whose right hand grasps John Sikobe's left hand. The circle is completed by John's right reaching out to Patrick's left. This is a historic circle; it has been forty years in waiting to happen! Praise the Lord! You are faithful.

Together again and expressing our love to our Savior and Lord! Just like in the old youthful days, our voices rise up to the heavens in supplication, worship and prayer to HIM who is able to do more than we think ask or imagine. The great I AM, the Creator of the heavens and earth, King of Kings and Lord of Lords, the Ancient of days. He is the One to whom all men run. He is worthy of all glory and honor.

Lord, thank you for friendship. Friendship sharpens us and brings us to the place of total surrender and dependence on our gracious God. Friendship is not temporal; it is eternal; one day we will sit on the other shores of glory land and tell the story of how we overcame. We are friends forever! Thank you Pat (Otis), Babu, Nick, Cyrus and many others for being our friends.

Beginnings for Flo

But there is more to the story. Let us look at Florence's side of the story to complete the picture of who we are. Florence Nolega was born into the Makindu family to Joseph Gwehona and Jonesi Lozenja Makindu on 24th September 1954. She was seventh amongst twelve siblings, five girls and seven boys. Florence was born in Eldoret, but spent her early years in their rural home in Maragoli, Viyalo, Igunga village. The Makindus were serious Quakers (Friends Church) and the children were brought up in the Quaker traditions and teachings. Florence took her faith seriously and tried to live up to her faith. With such a large family, which was not uncommon then, life for Florence was exciting with unity, loyalty and support for each other amongst the siblings that helped the family overcome many obstacles.

Tea Without Sugar: Chastened for a Destiny

Florence is non-violent in her approach to issues and through her early life she demonstrated an aversion to physical engagement with her age-mates. In fact it has always been said that Florence could not harm a fly. Her gentleness and love for others is clearly evident in her dealings. However, it is important to note a courageous determination to call people to account. She can easily and without delay confront issues. She is able to overcome her fear of a physical threat. This helps her find a solution immediately.

Her education began at the Igunga Primary School in their local village, just about five hundred meters from their home. Following successful completion of class seven where she did her Certificate of Primary Education (CPE), she enrolled in Asumbi Girls High School in South Nyanza. She did her 'O' Levels in 1972. In 1973 she took up an appointment with The Kenya External Telecommunications Corporation and was trained in telephone communication as an International Telephone Operator at Extelecom House, Nairobi.

Sometimes it is so romantic to imagine that God was preparing us for each other. Each one of us having a very different temperaments and experiences but being fitted for each other t. To be a team that could model the marriage relationship for His glory. In our small way we desired to be a blessing to many as they too walk through their marriage experience.

Starting Work, Courting Flo

When I had completed my 'A' Levels I was employed by Barclays Bank Kenya Limited as a Bank Clerk in March of 1975. My starting salary was Kshs. 880/= monthly. I still lived with my father and helped run the home.

My father attempted to convince me to go to the USA for further studies but I declined. I planned to go through the ranks of employment and take private studies in banking or accounting. My desire was to remain in Kenya rather than go to a far away land to study.

While hardly eighteen I had a declared dream to get married not later than the age of 24 years. I told anyone who cared to listen to me this desire. We married on 3rd March 1979 and I turned 24 the same month on 30th March 1979. My dream had been fulfilled.

Our courtship meeting in the bus had a life changing effect on me. In the evening I asked a friend to take me to Florence's home so that I could get to know her better. He knew the family since they came from the same village. I could have easily lost my heart as it pumped threateningly as if to pop out of my chest. This meeting at her home did not disappoint me at all. It confirmed her great beauty both of body and person. She proved adorable to me! My mind was made up, this was the girl who would become Mrs. Sikobe.

However, a few weeks after our bus encounter, I had a nasty run-in with her elder sister. That evening we were strolling in the estate with my buddy of many years Patrick Mutua. As we passed near Florence's flat I thought I saw her standing in the balcony. I decided to go upstairs to the third storey to look into the balcony with a cheery, "Hi Flo!" However, to my utter shock the lady whom I thought to be Flo was her elder sister. And she was expectant! One of the problems with the Makindu girls was that they could confuse you if you were not careful; they looked so alike! She tore into me with harsh words and abused me. She called out to Flo to tell her of the type of boys we were: manner-less boys who called out girls from balconies. That really got me upset and we stopped contact from then on for a few months.

We resumed our contact however following the encouragement of her sister in-law. I met her one evening at the Gill House bus stage waiting for the Nairobi South B bus. She told me to call Flo and gave me the number where Flo was now living with her sister; the same sister who had caused our separation! I called her that night and we spoke for a long time as if there had been no gap in time. We were now back together again!

There was however only one problem: Flo was not a born again Christian and therefore was not qualified to be my wife. You see, yours faithfully was the Chairman of the Youth at the Mariakani Christian Centre, Nairobi South B. It would have been inconceivable that I would introduce a non-believer to my Pastor as my fiancé. No way! I was a role model for the youth and that would not carry well with my testimony. At that time salvation was critical in any relationship. It meant separation from the world and its attractions. This was encapsulated in the chorus, "The things I used to do, I don't do them anymore x3 There is a great change since I have been born again."

Tea Without Sugar: Chastened for a Destiny

So what did we do? We agreed that we would not push the salvation agenda at all, and that Florence would regularly attend our Church and youth services. She was under no pressure to convert and our friendship would be just that; friendship.

In the scheme of life, it always seems to me that God has a game plan for our lives and that it is both detailed and for our own good. In fact it is in that scheme that all things are organized expressly to fit us for the purpose for which we were born. Florence, a beautiful, humble and disciplined girl brought up in the village of Igunga, Maragoli and John, a brash and loud boy from the urban world of estate gangs and partying: made for each other! How?

Together

Two young people from different backgrounds brought together by a binding attraction to each other through a chance meeting in a bus. Two young people had feelings for each other that were ready to overcome any obstacle. Two young people who had decided to have a godly courtship: a courtship that would encourage the youth. Two young people so much in love!

Our courtship lasted over two years. By the Lord's grace Florence received Christ on 23rd September 1977. We got married on 3rd March 1979. Yes, my dream of marriage at the age of 24 years old was actualized.

What has marriage meant to us? What lessons have we learnt? Sometimes I get the impression that I have had two calls in my life: number one call is unto salvation as a pastor, and number two is to marriage. Pastoring seemed to come naturally to me. A deep desire to be of help to others and looking out for their comfort has always been in me. Once I was able to understand the theological implications of what life is all about and felt my individual need for a defined purpose I realized my call was to be a pastor.

The Lesson of Helplessness

Every time we talk marriage we hear the Swahili phrase, 'Pingu ya maisha' (Prison for life) and never stop to consider the truth of the saying. It is assumed that the phrase seeks to warn the couple concerning the prison they are entering. Yet they seem to enter gladly with wide-open eyes! The marriage relationship is like no other; the intensity of emotions as we go through courtship, the innovative and creative atmosphere as one persuades the other with great charm, the employment of every weapon available in their arsenal to ensure they enter into the box and the feeling of invincibility, as in we can do all things together. And finally, the wedding happens. Wow, what a thrill!

Fast forward deep into marriage and you begin to see the many obstacles that one encounters in this crucible of testing called marriage. You soon realize that: We are held captive in the prison called marriage. We are walled in by societal expectations, born out of traditions and constrained by the invasion of new cultures and ways and ceremoniously tied in by the knot of covenantal vows. With death as the only door open to end the relationship each spouse is completely dependent on their mate in a-do-or-die embrace.

Marriage requires the mate to build the other into the fullness of their roles and potential. We float or sink together.

In our journey in marriage Florence and John have realized the joy of this imprisonment. The vows sounded very romantic as we declared it before the congregation; "I, John, take you Florence, to be my wedded wife, to have and to hold, from this day forward, for better, for worse, for richer, for poorer, in sickness and in health, to love and to cherish, till death do us part, or the Lord comes for His own, and hereto I pledge you my faithfulness."

In our rural setting in Western Kenya, calamities and sicknesses and all other bad things were chased away with great shouts and drumming to go to Lake Victoria to affect the people nearer the lake. We don't do that anymore since we have intermarried so much that it does not make sense to send calamities to your in-laws. Ordinarily, most of us believe that bad things should not happen to good people like us!

Our marriage vows are indicative of a readiness to tackle any and every challenge that we could encounter. Although our focus is hope in the good positive side of the vows we must be ready for the negative too.

As we have taken care of each other, in sickness and in health, we have learned one lesson; the lesson of helplessness. Sickness places one of us at the disadvantage of weakness and inability to care for self.

In many cases the sick spouse is totally dependent on the healthy partner for care. The healthy partner holds in their hand the power to dispense or withhold tender loving care (TLC).

At the beginning of our journey we elected to lay a foundation that would meet the challenges of the years ahead. We chose to be committed to each other no matter what. Through failings and disappointments we chose to learn lessons and exercise forgiveness and love regardless. Our steadfast hold onto our faith in the Lord Jesus Christ always seemed to carry the day for us. The Lord is always a cry away. Humility exercised in demanding situations ensured that our egos did not climb to lofty heights that would result in irreconcilable differences.

So what is this lesson in helplessness? Well the general lesson is to never hit your partner when they are down. They are in a state of helplessness and must look up to you to carry the load of marriage for the two of you.

So my Flo won't turn on her own, so I have to turn her; she cannot bath herself, so I will gladly bath her; she cannot eat on her own, so I will feed her patiently; she cannot engage the world around her to defend herself, so I will be around and don't you dare threaten her! If you try anything funny then you are a " gonna!" (Expression of the 70s meaning 'you are dead meat').

The Author of marriage in Genesis declared that the two become one. Earlier on in chapter one verse 27 we note that 'He created them male and female.' In chapter two a rib is extracted from Adam and Eve is made. They were one before they got distinctions of man and woman. In our walk in marriage we must always remain ONE IN TWO. Our visions, desires ambitions must become one. She is me and I am her. Hers is mine and mine is hers. Her helplessness is mine and my strength is hers. We are fated into oneness. We cannot escape this union. It is indivisible, what God has joined together let no man put asunder! This pretty well covers the vows. If you jump ship midway of your marriage journey for any reason other than what the vows stipulate then I suppose we can only expect dire consequences from the Author Himself. Let us remain committed to each other all the time. That is the expectation of our vows which is non-negotiable.

The ups and down of life have served to cement my faith in the

Lord. I remember Saturday 6th February 2010. We were so broke that we had not bought food for the house and diapers for Flo. I had to improvise by cutting off the dry ends of used diapers from the dustbin to make one that could hold out for the night. An earlier attempt to use a panty and toilet tissue ended up messing the bed.

This was one of the worst days of my life as a husband. I came face to face with the inability of a man to provide for his family, it was so painful! I had on previous occasions had to seek help from family and felt that I had become such a burden to them. I felt like a beggar and such a letdown. I cried a lot that day for experiencing the worst indignity a man can suffer in life: the inability to provide and care for his family. I remember Flo innocently asking me if I did not have Kshs. 600/= (the price of diapers) to buy diapers. It was excruciatingly painful to answer her innocent question. I love Flo, she is a blessing from the Lord! She is so supportive and so encouraging.

That was not the only time we experienced this indignity. Later in the same year in July, we had gone to Western Kenya for a burial of a relative over a weekend. We had only one diaper which was used on Saturday 17th during the day, Flo slept in it through the night. On Sunday morning I had to drain it (God is merciful: it was only urine) then wash it with hot water, drain it with a cloth and then use a lessos (fabric used to wrap around a woman to make a long skirt) to support it and dress Flo with it. You should have seen her knowing smile that beamed with grace and support. There were no complaints, just satisfaction that we were in it together and that God would see us through. We used a plastic mat to protect the car seat from soaking and drove the nearly 130kms back to Eldoret. That was quite an experience. So broke that we had no diapers and no medicine!

Our experience is that the Lord has always come through for us by way of divine provision. Even in the darkest hour of financial challenges, He has always ensured that we were provided for in time. Marriage requires that spouses put their trust in the Lord and avoid destructive discouragement and fear. The Lord is faithful and will come through for us. Health challenges also carry with them spiritual effects. One night Flo told me she was afraid of dying. She was convinced that she was soon going to die from her sickness. I had just shared with her the passing on of a young lady who was known to us. I was taken aback and regretted talking about death with her. On further inquiry I was shocked to find out that her real problem was that she was not sure that she would go to heaven! We took time together and discussed salvation. Are you saved, I asked? Yes, she responded. When? September, 1977. We then went through the Word to gain her assurance of salvation. I realized that it would be necessary to have a deliberate daily activity of the Word with her to build her hope and faith.

God again never disappoints. About ten days earlier a friend of ours had send a text message that said, "May the God of hope fill you with all joy and peace as you trust in Him, so that you may overflow with hope by the power of the Holy Spirit." That was so appropriate for our situation. God is indeed good and is always proactive where our lives and welfare are concerned. Hallelujah!

I realized that it would be necessary to have a deliberate daily activity of the Word with her to build her hope and faith.

God again never disappoints. About ten days earlier a friend of ours had send a text message that said, "May the God of hope fill you with all joy and peace as you trust in Him, so that you may overflow with hope by the power of the Holy Spirit." That was so appropriate for our situation. God is indeed good and is always proactive where our lives and welfare are concerned. Hallelujah!

The Lesson of Encouragement

The lesson of encouragement that has been consistent in our life is that God keeps our heads above the water. He saves us from going under due to the pressure of our challenges. Just before Flo had the fourth stroke on 29th September 2014, we had travelled a very fruitful journey to recovery from the third stroke of 7th October 2009. More than four arduous years of patience and expectation had gone by. Flo had been in Nairobi since March 2014 living with my brother Nicholas and his wife Elizeba for two to three months. She was attending physiotherapy sessions at Kenyatta National Hospital and at their home under their wonderful tender loving care together with Flo's sister Emmy who was always available to help. Flo came back to me in Eldoret having abandoned the wheelchair and attempting the use of a walking frame to move around. Oh Praise the Lord! Halleluyah! God had done us great good. Now we could picture FloJo as a couple walking together going about their business on their feet. Our joy was visible and complete.

Then on 29th September all that was wiped away by another stroke! We were devastated! How could this be? Could we not be given a break from the challenge of sickness for a bit?

Divine Healing

One of the most difficult questions to answer is, 'You are a pastor, and you believe in God, why then has God not healed your wife Flo?' Divine healing is a topic that always springs up when we have health challenges. It always seems that everyone expects pastors to procure healing on demand for their families and for themselves.

I remember 13th April 2012, Flo had been very uncomfortable from about 1.27am and appeared unable to sleep with breathing difficulty and itchiness on the legs, I had prayed for an hour plus and applied powder to ease the itching. I was tired and thought, 'She has been sick for too long. Surely God is able to heal her?'

Wonders never cease! The following morning we visited a herbal clinic to which we had been referred. This was in complete contrast to my question during the night! Was this going to be God's way of healing Flo? At the herbal clinic we met the doctor who took us through a diagnosis of the disease and how the treatment regime would work. It sounded good until he told us the cost of the treatment. It would last 8-12 months and at a cost of Kshs. 10,200/= per month! Surely!!

Then it dawned on me that as a child of God, God is our healer, He has already paid in full for the healing on Calvary's tree, could I not call on His name for her healing and total deliverance? I then decided that I must take charge of the situation and act with authority in Jesus name.

Following this experience the only prudent approach to our health challenges seemed to lie in trusting in God for healing and sustenance. I decided that we would have to throw ourselves at the mercy of the Lord and refuse to be frightened by the various manifestations of attacks on us. We needed to make prayer our first port of call when such attacks reared their head and stand firm in His promises.

The pain that we experience in sickness can hopelessly convolute the issue of divine healing and reduce faith in God's word. It causes us to seek for help as if we were clutching for straws to save us from drowning. Fear truly hath torment.

I believe in divine healing. In my time as a pastor I have seen people healed firsthand and heard testimonies that have been validated concerning healing. There is no doubt at all. In one of our services at Springs of Hope Eldoret God healed a sister who was deaf and dumb. She had been in our employment at the Blossom School for some years. It was instant and a great thing to witness! Medical practice has its place in healing although as an industry it has a high level of both malpractice and greed for money. This tends to make it too expensive for the majority of people and at times opens them to rogue professionals and quacks. The most disappointing aspect of healing is when Christians place all their faith in man and neglect to trust God. I have witnessed a total lack of faith in God's power of healing even for mild situations and a blind trust in what the doctor says. This attitude borders on a declaration of our God being unable to heal as per His promise.

But He is surely able. Up to now God has not healed Flo. I continue to sit by her side, waiting, trusting, believing. We are His.

John is now a retired pastor who oversees two churches. He completed his degree at Discipleship College in November 2013 among the last group to graduate from Lee University.

EPILOGUE: A LAST SIP OF TEA
D. E. "Gene" Mills, Jr.

"They will be called oaks of righteousness, the planting of the Lord, to display his glory. They shall build up the ancient ruins, they shall raise up the former devastations; they shall repair the ruined cities, the devastations of many generations." (Isaiah 61 3b-4, NRSV)

One of the incredible things about the action of God in the world of humanity is the way in which God takes things that are overlooked and discounted by people and uses them for his glory. Things which are inconsequential on their own, people who have very inauspicious beginnings, God takes and uses in ways which are often mind-boggling to us. Events which some have meant for our harm, and even incredibly ignorant and destructive choices we have made, become the ingredients which are used to build God's active reign in the world. Each one of the stories in this powerful book is evidence of the ways in which the grace, love, and power of God are alive in East Africa.

The scripture at the heading of this epilogue is a statement about the ways in which those who were previously downtrodden become the active agents in restoration and revitalization of a people and a land. It is the continuation of the scripture which Jesus used to announce his earthly ministry in the synagogue in Nazareth (Luke 6). What Jesus came to do was to reach into the places that the religious and powerful were unwilling to go and to make something beautiful and powerful as a testimony to his goodness. Or as the beginning of verse 3 in the Isaiah passage says, "to give them a garland instead of ashes, the oil of gladness instead of mourning, the mantle of praise instead of a faint spirit." The "instead of" is powerful! What is natural in the world – the world where these testimonies were born – is that poverty, disease, crime, abandonment leads to a silent, quick, and cheap death. The natural path is hopelessness. Nevertheless, God's grace reaches in and provides an "instead of" that changes everything.

These former students of Discipleship College, graduates and those waiting for their final paperwork to clear, are now out there standing as "oaks of righteousness" rebuilding and restoring a hurting people. As you see in their stories, their passion is born out of the own lives. Their pain and struggle leads to ministries of healing. Their drive toward making an impact is accomplishing just that: communities are being changed life-by-life. This sampling of testimonies show a people who are not willing to sit down and do nothing while those around them are going through pain and heartache with which they are intimately familiar. They stand up and actively work out the love of God. Despite many opportunities in the past – they have not given up because the road is too long or the burden too heavy. Through the strength of the Spirit, the burden has become light.

This passion for ministry is also impacted by their training here at Discipleship College. Out of nothing just a few short years ago, this institution was born in order to train people in ministry skills, to establish solid biblical and theological belief structures, and to help shape true Christ-like character. Just as these individual ministers who are working in a variety of capacities are now standing in their worlds in a different light, so is the college as we stand on the verge of great new horizons.

This book is the tangible expression of what we here at the college are trying to accomplish for the reign of God in the world. As the new Director/President at the college, I am privileged to have become a part of this community. The more recent of these students have sat in my classroom and worshipped with me in chapel. I have forever been changed by their stories. Their passion for God and the power in their narratives are an inspiration to me to be better in everything I do. I learn from them and the students who are following after them even as I teach and lead.

I pray the same for you!

D. E. "Gene" Mills, Jr.
Eldoret, Kenya
January 2012

GLOSSARY OF TERMS

A Levels — These levels are equivalent to the first two years of college and are sometimes called forms 5 and 6. These levels are no longer required in the Kenyan system, having been replaced by college.

A.I.C. — African Inland Mission has started many churches in Africa which are now called African Inland Churches.

Ampath — An HIV/AIDS research and treatment facility in Eldoret which is considered the foremost center for such research in Africa. Patients not only receive free medication but they also learn how better nutrition can increase their changes of survival. The facility was started by a man named Dr. Mamlin in cooperation with Indiana University and Moi University Hospital (a Kenyan government hospital named after a former president of Kenya).

Bhangi — Opium

Baraza — Community council meeting where everyone in the community is allowed to have a voice, to speak out on an important issue.

Bursary — Monetary reward given by an institution to help a student complete his education.

Care-front — This term originated with a man named David Augsberger in his book, *Caring Enough to Confront: How to Understand and Express Your Deepest Feelings to Others*, 1980. Dr. Marcia Andersno further explored this term in her 2006 book, *Carefrontation: Dare to Face the Goliath, Care Enough to Confront*.

Cassava — Root of a plant that is used to make tapioca

CD4 — A CD4 count is a method used to determine the progress of an HIV/AIDS positive person. CD4 cells are the lymphocytes most targeted by HIV/AIDS and as the disease progresses they decrease in number.

Chapatis — Flat, wheat bread, originating in India, brought to Kenya by the indentured Indian laborers brought to Kenya by the British.

CIMS — Certificate in Ministerial Studies, a program developed by the Church of God, Cleveland, Tennessee to train ministers. The program utilizes DVD's and a local facilitator who guides students in discussing the material in the Kenyan context.

CRE — Christian Religious Education

Dinka — A tribe in South Sudan. There are various groups within the Dinka tribe, including Bor, Rek and others. The Dinka were a primary group fighting for the independence of Southern Sudan. Independence was finally granted through referendum in July, 2011, after more than 20 years of war with the Moslem-dominated North Sudan.

Dowry — Typically cattle, sheep, goats, etc., given by a man to the family of the woman he intends to marry to show his determination to marry her and to provide faithfully for her.

Emboka — A type of amaranthus, edible greens

Forms 1,2,3,4 — These grades are equivalent to U.S. high school: freshman, sophomore, junior and senior years.

IDP — Internally displaced persons. This refers to 150,000 persons who fled their homes in the 'clashes' of 2008 between tribes in Kenya.

FISH Media — The acronym stands for Fishing for the Lost and Feeding the Found. This organization has a radio station and is headed by a blind evangelist and musician, Reuben Kigame.

Githeri   A kikuyu dish made of boiled beans and corn.

Jaggery   Traditional, unrefined, non-centrifugal, whole cane sugar. It is a concentrated product of cane juice without separation of molasses and crystals.

Jeanette Chesser   American missionary who impacted the college, especially with her teachings concerning the Holy Spirit, as an adjunct faculty at college over a period of four years.

Jembe   Hoe

Jerikan   Square 5 gallon can used for such things as oil or gasoline.

KAG   Kenyan Assemblies of God.

Khaki   Rough, cotton shirt

Kakuma Refugee Camp   This camp in northern Kenya has refuges from several East African Countries including Ethiopia, Sudan, Uganda, Rwanda and Somalia. The largest group, however, have come from war-torn South Sudan.

Kayaba   Prickly fence, often cactus or some other plant that would be very unpleasant to run into.

KCPE   Kenyan Certificate of Primary Education exams. Kenyan education is based on the model introduced by the British. At the completion of every level of education, comprehensive exams are given to determine the student's fitness to proceed to the next level.

KCSE   Kenyan Certificate of Secondary Education exams. A student must attain a grade of C+ to be able to proceed to university. The government determines who will study certain subjects. For example those who have a grade of A can study medicine, etc.

Kesha	Overnight prayer meetings. It is related to the word, 'kesho' which means tomorrow.
Lorry	Truck
Makuta	Palm-type branches (Dinka Bor language)
Maram	Clay soil and rocks especially good for making roads
Mason cap	Masons (brick layers) cover their heads with a hat made from the paper cement bags to keep cement dust out of their ears, eyes and nose.
Mau Mau fighters	Kikuyu tribesmen who revolted against British rule in 1952 and 1960. It finally lacked widespread support and was put down by the British.
Mzee	Swahili for old man, actually it is used for a man once he is married. Before that he is a boy. When he marries, he is an old man!
O Levels	These levels are equivalent to forms 1,2,3,4. This terminology was used when Kenya offered both A levels (forms 5 and 6) and O levels (forms 1-4).
Papyruis	A thin paper-like material made from the pith of the papyrus plant, a wetland sedge.
Panga	Machete
Parade	Assembly time for school children, usually held outside
PEFA	Pentecostal Evangelical Fellowship of Africa
Pombe	Local beer
Prefect	A student who is chosen because of excellent performance, both academically and in deportment to be an assistant to the teacher in the classroom.
Primary	In Kenya, primary grades are now grades 1-8. At the time of some of these stories primary education was only

grades 1-7.

Pyrethum Dried flower heads from a plant used to make insecticides.

Rescue Center An interdenominational center on the outskirts of Eldoret which seeks to rescue street children and rehabilitate them, either returning them to their parents or places them in Children's Homes in the city. At present there are approximately 70 boys and girls in this facility.

Safari Bed Small folding, travel bed

Shamba A small amount of land on which food stuffs are planted for the sustenance of a Family. Typically such things as maize and sukuma wiki are grown there. It is very important that every man have a shamba, not only for growing food but also as a place of burial. It is also important that one build at least a small house and outhouse there.

Simsim Small seeds (sesame seeds)

Slowly by slowly This expression is a common one used by Kenyans and is a direct translation of their 'pole pole' which means that something happens a little at a time or gradually.

Small father This term refers to an uncle. Because he is the younger brother of one's father, he is called the 'small father.'

SPLA/M Sudan People's Liberation Army/Movement is the rebel army which managed to bring the Sudan situation to a referendum.

Standard 1-8 Primary education levels are called 'standards' rather than grades.

Starehe This is a secondary school in Nairobi which is considered

	one of the best in the country for poor but bright students who desire to have an education.
Sukuma wiki	'Push through the week' This term is given to kale (or collard greens) which is friend with onions and tomatoes and steamed. This nutritious and inexpensive vegetable is usually eaten with *ugali* and helps the person have something substantial to eat for the rest of the week when one's salary is all used up.
TSC	Teacher's Service Commission is a government body which licenses teachers and provides teachers to various schools throughout the country.
Ugali	A basic staple made from maize flour by boiling it in water until it forms a self-standing mass which can be pinched off in the hand, rolled in a ball or formed into a 'spoon' with a thumb print to hold another food such as *sukuma wiki*.
UT	Untrained teacher. This is someone who is given a job as a teacher without formal training. This is generally a temporary measure.
Wazungu	Swahili word for Europeans (plural for Mzungu)
Woova wa jela	Prison salvation